The Theatre of War

Dr. Boban Ramesan

ISBN: 978-1-923679-14-6 (ebook)
ISBN: 978-1-923679-15-3 (paperback)

DEDICATION

"To
The blood and tears of the innocents …"

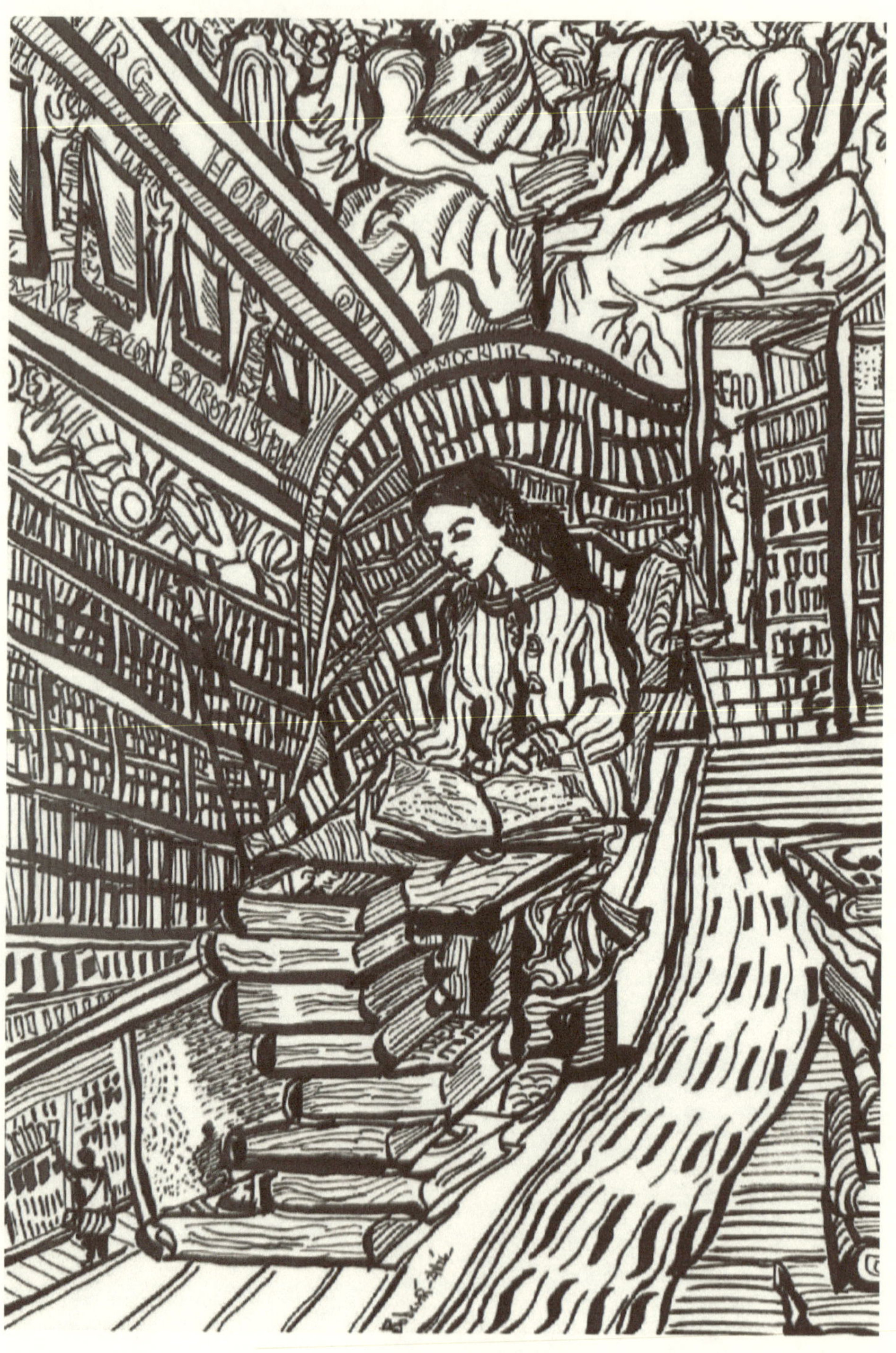

VIRGIL
HORACE
OVID
BYRON SHELLEY
PLATO
DEMOCRITUS
READ

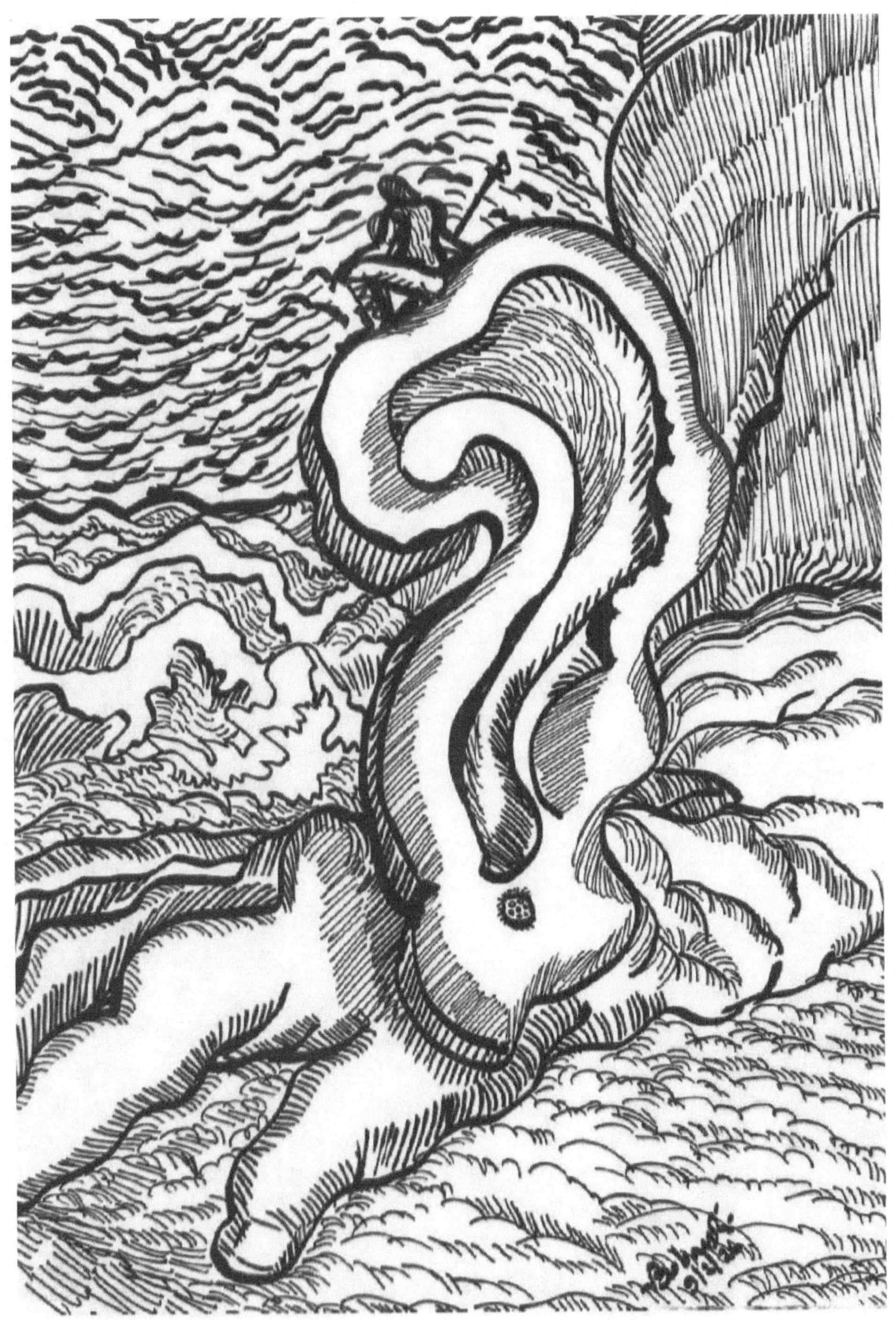

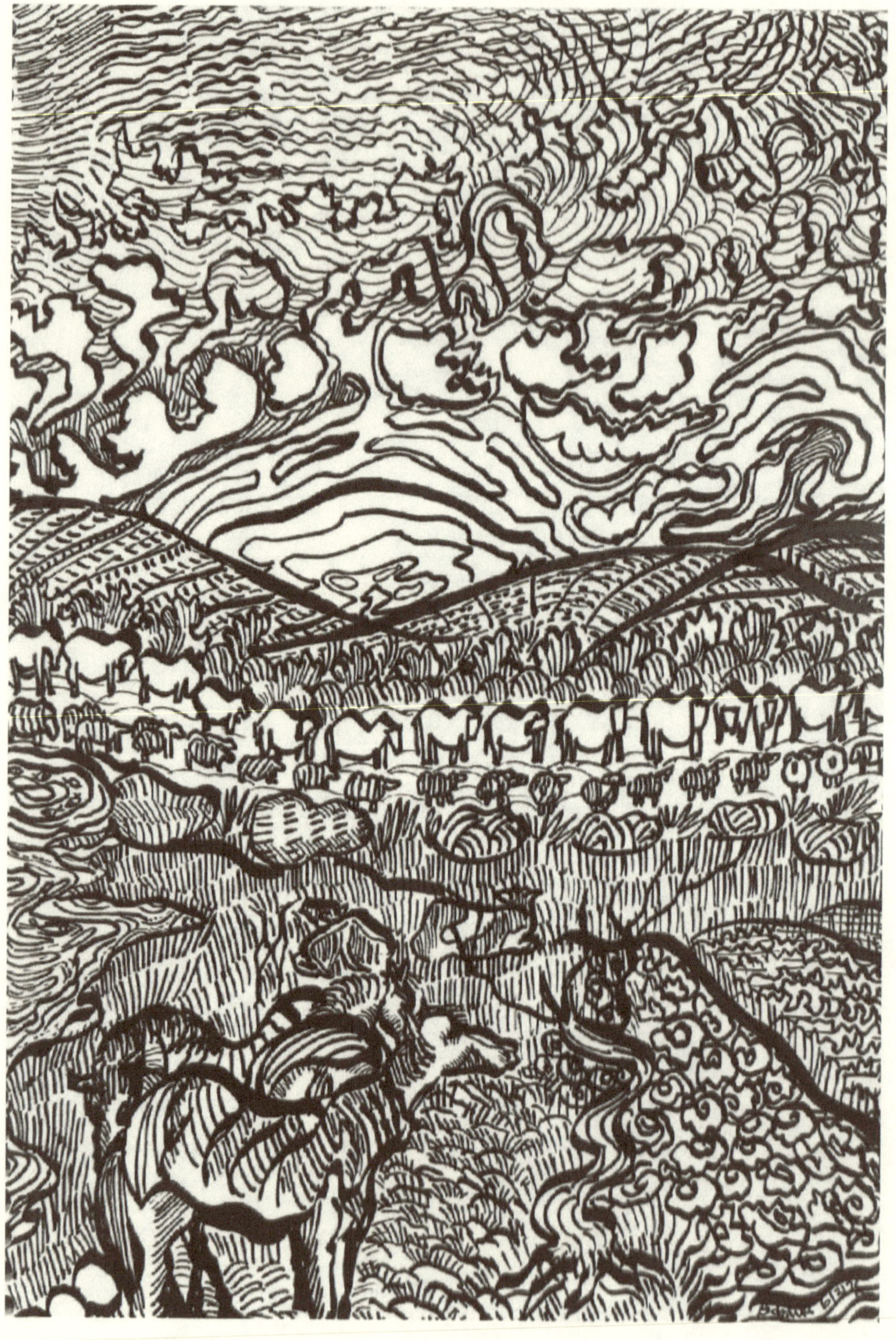

"Men grow tired of sleep, love, singing and dancing sooner than of war…"

~ Homer

CONTENTS

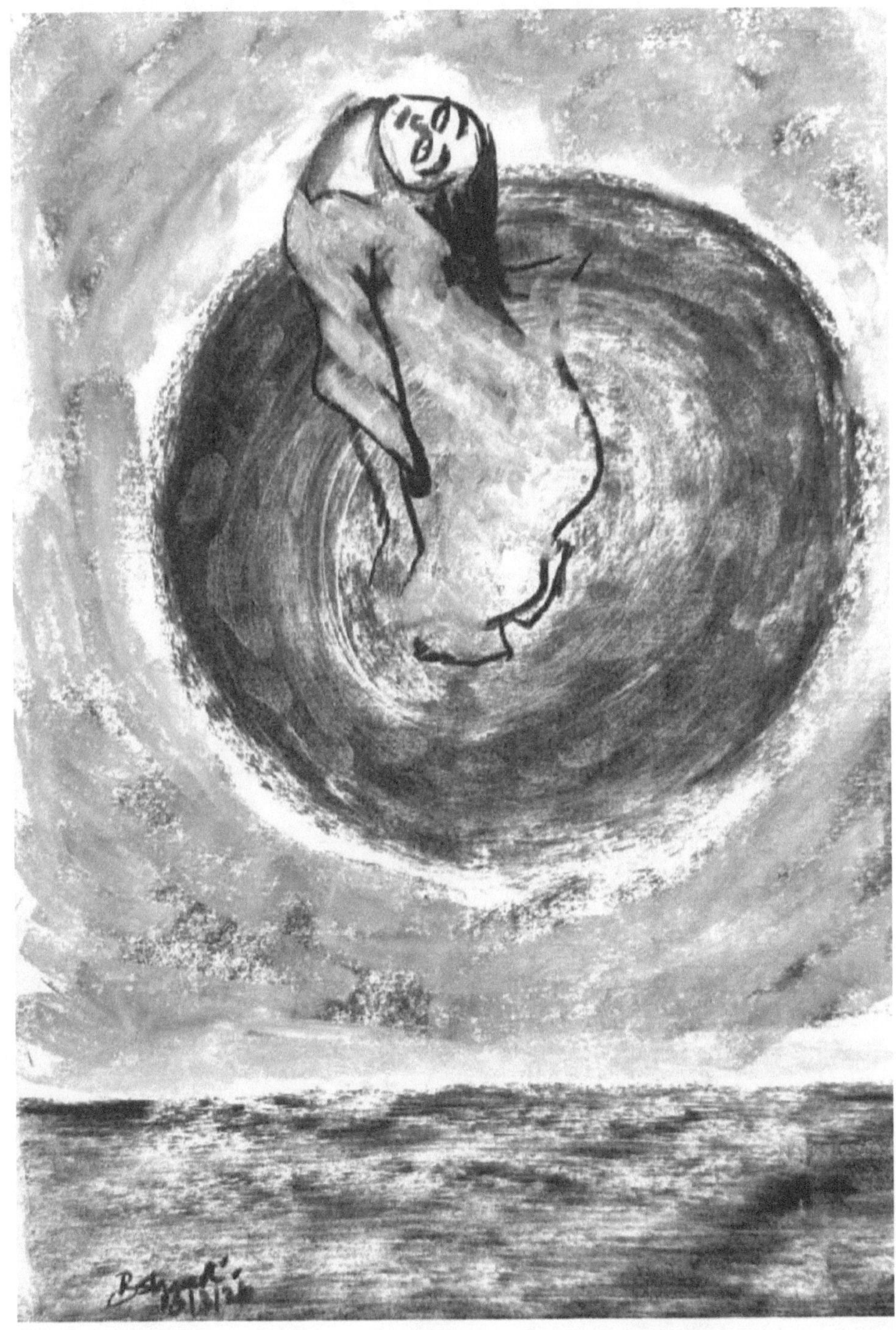

A CONVERSATION

"Do you want to be a caveman?"

Asked God nonchalantly

I looked with askance

At the unexpected question

Here he was!

Exploring my ambitions

Even without my knowledge

"I am in love

With my city

My belongings

I'm in love

With the concept of love itself "

I exclaimed

Stunned by my own honesty!

The God listened

With his eyes closed

("Vision curtains the truth "

I remembered the saint's words)

"My travelogue is long

Rich and eventful,

I'm on the opposite shore

Of regression,

Civilised over time

With evolutionary wisdom,

I've no nostalgia for the times

Of life in the cave

As I haven't lived in it …

("Nostalgia is after all a memory

Sweetened by pain of loss ")

Was he all ears for my mumblings?

I believe so, blindly but truthfully!

"I can see myself in a picture

As a nude caveman

With bloodied meat on his spear

His tastebuds tantalised

By the smell of warm blood!"

(After an unsettling pause)

"That's what I fear

The man (within me!)

Who belongs to the Stone Age?

But has never really been dead,

Who lives in the psyche?

And can do the unimaginable,

Cruel when judged by modernity,

An ape that was losing its identity

Transforming into something else,

A hairy monster, with a heart

That had begun to feel

The entanglement of emotions

And the trap of the web of life …"

I don't know the reason for my eloquence

But there was a genuine feeling in it

As the God slept in the sea of the cosmos…

"The threat of insanity

Is what I dread the most?

Was the caveman sane after all?

A violent birth, a soulless creature

That was just beginning to learn

About the darkness he found himself in …"

"Thought is a pain,

It is the opening to a wound

And once he learnt to think

The world must've been even more painful,

Fragile, meaningless, obscure …

The blood from the wound

Was not appetising,

Thought wasn't the food

For his starving body

Yet it compelled him to believe

That he was special,

A being (probably) with a soul,

With a peculiar armour of the senses

That extended his awareness

From his self to the limitless

And fathomless skies, and beyond …"

Did the God give out a smile?

Or was it just another illusion?

("The antidote to the innate imperfection

Is what creates the imaginative space")

"The caveman had relationships

Fathering children, many of them,

With very few survivors,

He copulated with virulence

As if to counter the uncaring nature,

How could a mother be so apathetic?

Unmoved by the tears and wails of loss?"

"The man was aware of his forefathers

And he too would become one,

A monument in stone from the Stone Age,

With the scattered graffiti of edicts

Over his lifeless body,

They said he was held the divine torch

Though he knew he was nothing but darkness …"

Should I be philosophising to God himself?

I withdrew into a shell at that thought,

But words flew from my mouth

Like flocks of uncaged birds …

("The voice of the dispossessed celestial

That implodes with the agony of abandonment ")

"Nothing was angelic or pristine

Benevolence, the most supreme of all virtues

Came through much later,

With the patchy comfort of society

And mutual caring, with a moral pact

That man knew not where he got it from!"

"Goodness, is it evil in disguise,

With a visual appeal but with no substance?

The pathology of the mind

And its staggering invisibility

Puts man in a state of perpetual despair,

If only he could sedate his anxieties

And feel free, he thinks,

That's the dilemma of being "myself "

Untrue, encumbered with prejudices

Unable to take on the burden

Of disturbing truths anymore …"

"The one who aspires to be a tree

Doesn't even become a leaf,

Death is weightless

Devoid of the lofty heights of fame,

Sinking into the hole of oblivion,

Seeking burial in forgetfulness …"

I'm talking to silence

An unseen wall stood between us,

Man, and his God

"It's an endless hole of leaves

Falling down with grace

Knowing not about the floor

As life has ended,

So too has the consciousness,

The tracks aren't serpiginous anymore

But united into a single line

For the leaves to follow

Conveyed across the prism of time

Into the volume-less space

Of unsweetened endings …"

"The fictional fantasy

In which man himself is a character

Masquerades as reality,

The same fallibility of the caveman

Lives through the generations,

As men fight for that evasive space

That they believe to be real

But essentially a powerful illusion

With the magnetism to deceive

The intellect, virtually creating a cave

From which modern man cannot escape!…"

I could not hide my own bewilderment

At such a discovery

"The caveman is not prehistory

Nor is it an idea

But a reality of the modern world,

His strong sinews still exist

Full of rage and craving for power

Stubbornly keeping man entrapped

Within an incredulous gossamer

Of emerging dreams

And submerged memories …"

I was like a newborn

Feeling the first ray of sun

Birthed from the hermitage:

"The wisdom of spirituality

Ought to be the wisdom gained

From the act of living within chaos,

The cave is not a monastery

For a quiet meditative experience,

But a bloodied foul smelling space

With discarded afterbirth(s)

And human excrements,

The partly consumed bones of beasts

And the insatiable pangs of hunger "

I paused to take a breath:

"The caveman is not a sage

Seeking sanctity in confinement,

He is an animal, aspiring to be a man,

A mythical creature with a hidden tail

A demon born to a god!…"

"He is not what he is

But what he wants to become,

He is not the paragon of virtues

Or the apostle of peace,

But a modicum of darkness

That is aware of what it is,

That which yearns for the light

That's encapsulated in infinity,

He is the poison of destruction

And the panacea of his own ills,

He is the admirer of love

A devotee of higher ideals,

But one who knows his inadequacies

And the eternal paradox that he is …"

What does one read from silence?

The holy book of eternity?

There aren't any words,

There are no optic symbols,

God was silent

I could read into it by myself

Not as a body but as a soul

That is transcendent, a cosmic principle

Then a member of the earthly world …

"The caveman could read, in that sense

Delving into the unfathomable silence,

The semantics and verbiage evolved

Not as substitutes for silence

But as tools to understand it

And the darkness within the being …"

"He would write his autobiography

On the walls of his cave

With the pigments from nature

And the ink of his own blood;

The conversation was honest

Between the man and the rock

Without the medium of language,

Co-authored by his own shadow "

("Could God have a shadow of his own image?

Is that man, as signalled by the lores?")

"It transpires that the caveman

Tried to reach out to a creator,

An incognito in the ebullient skies,

He must have been heart broken

That his cries went unheard,

Equally true that his grief was boundless

Before he importuned the invisibles…

Beleaguered by the temptations and the sins

The contraptions of ambiguous morals,

And the oneiric labyrinths of sleep,

He screamed, with a contorted face

To be heard, in the depths of the canyons

And the towering silhouettes of the heavens

As the plea of the restless caveman,

Febrile with the passion to live

And the concealed fear of death …"

At the mention of death, god smiled

Like a human being in sublime happiness

A thin veil of morning fog fell off the face

Revealing a solid piece of rock,

Without a trace of any sculpture

Or the touch of a human hand …

("Probably the most original of all arts

Isn't of human making ")

"The fissures have miniature lives

Nameless, mostly inconspicuous

Yet they have their own stories

Of cohabitation with the caveman,

Loneliness is but a human condition

A tangible perception of the mind

That is true as well as untrue …"

The stoic expression of the rock

Rendered a divine feeling to it

"The profoundness of loneliness

Is the basis of the scream?

That murmurs in the craters of the planets

To which life is alien and imperceptible "

""I" have woken up from a sleep

Within a deep cavernous space,

"I" have seen animals and birds

Amongst many nameless things,

Curious monuments of creativity,

Which spoke to "me" in my language;

But, all along it was a soliloquy,

"I" was conversing with myself

Like a winged creature trapped

In the interiors of imagination;

That's is the metaphor of life

All that exists within non-existence

A beautifully enchanting illusion

A gossamer that invites the soul

To spend a fraction of time on earth!

"I" do not exist in wakefulness

The self of the dream has become infinity

The self of the day is in the "now "of things

To partake in the activities of life,

Racing towards the sun for boundless energy

Before dying at nightfall, to be a dream

That dreams of the character with the self

As a participant in the evolving saga;

Magical are the illusions of light

That harbours one in make-believe tents

Where the ancients feel the present

And the future is alchemised with care;

"I" am an ingredient of that process

That is evolutionary and hard earned,

The soul of the music that fills the night

Comes from the reed of the vagrant mind,

As a passing tribute to the lost times,

"I" have been there, and will be there

In the yeti to be born cells of the future,

As a musical string of flowing water

Or the intriguing whisper of a breeze …"

For a moment I felt that

The self may be the god in the rock

And though the winds swept the hills and flew away

The feeling only grew stronger within me

""I" have come here to know, that's my only purpose

To know before my time comes,

In this vestibule of darkness, knowledge is everything

To follow the light trickling through the crevices

To reach the unknowable …"

The waters know "me", for I recognise them

As a part of being myself,

The sun is more than familiarity or friendship

What sustains a man on earth is not bonding of blood

But by the mysterious elements of nature,

The nature is within my'self',

As the mother of all those elements that make "me",

I'm a form of synthesised matter,

That has evolved from the unknown factors

Adding another layer to the suspense

That enshrouds the pyramid of life …"

The physical entity seemed unmoved

Though one cannot see the mind of a rock,

A flock of birds flew past the horizon

Around the red diamond of a star

"The mother's womb is a cave

So are the woods, with lives breathing within?

The myriad forms, as if it's purposeful

For a life to be lead in the darkness of a cave

Till the time to release into eternity,

Where the skies crumble like paper

And the earth a dot from the ink of God"

"The catacombs perspire with afterlives

As monuments of human ambitions,

The sleep is deep in the marble mausoleum

As the decayed bodies turn into dust,

The souls find peace in the cosmos

Seeking a creator of the consciousness

That has defined the impression of life…"

("No life is fully born till death")

"What's the truth of the being, the matter?

The solidness of flesh and bones

Innervated and sinewed, supplied with blood,

Dissipated into the atmosphere as nothingness

After the tenure is well and truly over?"

The particles move within the rock

Unseen and unheard, relentlessly

With rigour and rhythm,

The timelessness of space

And the innate musicality of the lives

Appearing and vanishing all around me

Put me in a state of enchantment,

Like a luminescent fly entering freely

Into the smorgasbord of fantasies …

"The caveman was the most original

Of all philosophers, who touched the very core?

Of life through his precarious existence,

His emotions were untrammelled, his perceptions not skewed

By the nonorganic mask of civility,

His life was not just about evading death

But to be felt by the downpours

And see the grandeur of the universe through naked eyes…"

The colours swam across the skies

Reflecting the irrevocable translation of life

From one to the next, and beyond

Straining the visually drenched eyes

"They celebrate the art of writing

And the art of reading the book,

The visual art of the caveman needs no preface

But the fine rock engraving is demanding

The keenest of attention from the beholder

To grasp the beautiful depth of the strokes

And the manifold interpretations that evolve

Multiplying the illusions with the light,

Unlike the reader who can toy with the words

The beholder subjects his entire senses to test

As he gazes at the ancient bison draped in blood

Rebirthing itself into life through the hiatus of time …

The caveman is an idea, so is his art

He's the seed of civilisation, the essence of humanity,

His face has the bruises of the violence of survival,

The congealed blood traverses the veins

Of the cave walls, as modernity implodes

Into mutations exponentially more violent

Than the most volatile of the cavemen!…"

The valley below was buzzing with lives

Reptiles with tentacles, beasts with great horns,

Extinct giants walking outside the frame of time;

I wasn't sure whether the god knew them,

Could they've preceded the birth of a creator?

The assembly of "the uncreated "was fascinating

"Things "before the consciousness of the cosmos

Could that even be possible?…

"The man must have thought

The night was not an absence of light, he felt

As loneliness gripped the imperilled life,

Thinking was primeval, the property of the intellect

Which made him distinctive from the rest of the world,

It composed his concept of self

Woven from the straws of his experience

And the ink of his own imagination"

"The end of the world would be a new beginning

When the caveman would be a germinal thought

With the entire civilisation condensed into a capsule

Of memory within that spark in the intellect;

And then he might start afresh

Not with bloodied violence, but with satire,

As a refined uncomplicated being

Who has realisation of his self

And has awareness of his mental faculties

Right from the beginning of his journey;

But that might be a non-human offshoot

Who cannot panic or collapse into grief,

Indifferent to loss and the pains of life

And less concerned about self-preservation,

Making him too open and vulnerable

To the dangers that would remain unchanged,

It would plant him at the epicentre of conflict

Between free will and the self,

The facets of his mind confused by his nonchalance …

The splintered subgroup of the species

Would be a new specimen, phenotypically human

But a caveman who has sublime artistic tastes

Who is essentially a nonviolent organism?

His aggressiveness replaced with complacency,

His ambition a remote unrealistic dream,

He wouldn't be the forefather of the dreamer

As his visions would be entombed in his art alone …

He would've have no inkling of progress

Instigated by the fear of abandonment,

The anxiety of being left behind by the tribe

That prefers to move on, neglecting the crippled;

But is that benign nature harmful?

Most probably not, though it's debatable

Whether the project of humanity would be fruitful

If it is shorn of the desires and passions

That relentlessly reshape and reconstruct

The fountain heads of advancements …"

The peregrinations of thoughts

Along the misty terrains of existence

Where the mud houses began to appear

As the wheel of civilisation turned

Brought a divine grace to the rock,

God too was evolving alongside man,

As the second shadow, unseen by light

Revealing himself only in the depths of darkness,

As a metaphysical metaphor of humanity,

Resilient and capable of unleashing wrath

Replicating the subconscious psyche of man…

"The caveman's life is an alluring fruit

In the tree of memory in the void,

What he has seen is the flesh of his life

It vanishes with the passing of light

The seed stays, with the aura of life

As a reflected memory, a solitaire

That shines bright, though illusionistic ..."

"Life's a sensory experience

A product of conflicting randomness,

A tribute to the ineffable love

Is at the heart of the living experience,

A singularity that evolves from the clutter

Of apparently unrelated factors,

It's a fateful coincidence,

The fusion of gametes of strangers

To beget the embryo of novelty,

That would evolve further into a human

Unlike any other, extant or expired,

Though the trajectory shares similarities

With that of the ancestor, the caveman,

Who was never satiated by his space?

And set out in search of his dreams,

To live in yet another wilderness

In the midst of uncertainty and fear;

There's something in him

That compels him to embrace the adventure,

Of being lost in the dense woods of anonymity,

Just so that he could find his soul

In the mythical aura of the transience,

He is but an insect that wilfully journeys

Towards the fire, knowing it is not just light

But the gaping mouth of death itself …"

The cosmos doesn't have any politics

But the heavens do, with warring gods

At each other's neck with their petty egos,

The replica of the complex human psyche,

Intelligent but with an unstable temperament

Decoying the frivolous lives into a promise

Of the eternity of a clouded paradise!

I was sounding out my own fears

As the god in the rock was all ears:

"Men were born from fish like creatures,

Everything belongs to the waters

And the waters in turn belong to nothingness…

Is it a playground or a battleground?

Where life comes face to face with death?

Is there a confrontation at all

Or it just a timely unconditional surrender?

Man tries to hold his ground firm

With his armamentarium of scientific tools

Unwilling to give up in the face of crisis,

And striving to make his life bearable;

Yet he suffers immensely and weeps profusely

At the realisation of loss after the battle is over

He delves in deep into his wounded psyche

As the fog gets denser restricting his vision,

The path subdivides into many

And he is at a loss unable to find his way …"

"What else has the caveman begot?

Apart from his accrued wealth of experiences

With the painful tales of troubles

The passions of love and immense despair?

His cave room was small in space

But he had plenty of room to think

His intellect throwing sparks of insights

Into the uncertainty that engulfed him;

His was a primitive journey, a beginning

Towards the attainment of the self,

The walls would become mirrors at night

To show to him the shades of his trueness,

A strange beast with tenderness in its eyes

Would stare back at him with surprising familiarity,

He had to create the imageries on the walls

Outlining the figures on the make-shift mirrors,

The ancestors conversed through the dreams

About the world they hoped for, and the lives they lost,

As the cosmic phenomenons continued unperturbed

By the travails of humans on the planet

Mere ants on the pale blue dot…

All was to pass into the realm of nothingness

Every drop of sweat was meant only for life on earth

Beyond that nothing existed in reality,

Over the course of time he would come to suspect

The originality of his own existence,

Horrendous were the tribal battles and bloodshed

"He" was worser than the roaming beasts

As he had the intellect they didn't possess,

Yet, he was more violent, despite the power of reason,

He was a shadow, that had a life of its own,

Parallel to what existed in the eyes of others,

He was a trifle in the trickeries of the passing light,

An illusion, nothing more, a thoughtful shadow

In a world which was steeped in darkness..."

"Did the caveman have any sense of music?

He must have, else he wouldn't be human,

For, art and music are inseparable,

Nature has her innate sublime poetry

Eons before the origins of language,

The analogy would be that of a newborn

That has the cerebral potential to be nurtured

And brought to full bloom over the years,

The caveman had everything that makes one human,

But, would that mean that language is an accessory,

A useful tool to bond people together,

Or is it the very foundation of humanity?

As some would say," the brick of civilisation is the word baked in the
kilns of intellect "

The man in the den communicated with his eyes

He must have felt the verbal urge on his tongue

But he was in the pre-linguistic times,

Where he found meaning in the symbols

Coined by his mind through the process of thinking;

He found ink in the colour of pigments

Art was his first step to literature,

So was the expression through dance

As the mellifluous music flowed from the reeds

And the drumheads covered in animal hide!

It follows that the language of every being

Is his own life with all its peculiar shades?

It is not just the verbiage, but a whole spectrum

Of expressions from thoughts to bodily movements,

Even the dead would communicate

Through the medium of silence,

The most powerful of all languages …

So, the caveman had his own language

Of visual symbols and abstract expressions

That exteriorised the meaning within the things

Then affixing a particular meaning to something;

Life was not to be lived without input

From the intellect of the human being,

To be fruitful it had to be meaningful

And the hidden meaning was extracted

Through the powerful tool of thoughts …"

The patches coalesce into oneness

A darkness sublime and deep

Subsuming the world in its entrancing effect,

The shadows are painted on the walls

Tall, convoluted, mysterious figures

The earthly children of the distant light,

Whilst god sleeps in an unbreakable vow,

A pact with nature for nonintervention;

The rock knows not the crises of mankind

But is cognisant of the predicament

That bridges god and humans alike,

The existence of both entities intertwined

By the lack of certitude on earth

And the assurance of mythical salvation

In the remotest cloud-wrapped heavens,

The poetic answer to the unanswerable things

That enshroud the gist of life …

"What if the caveman was born with fire?

In his fully grown and strong hands?

If the cave was a silky soft meadow

With sumptuous orchards within it,

He would have been something else,

He wouldn't become a human being,

Man wouldn't grow in his dreamy paradise,

A world devoid of pains and losses

Stunts his thoughts and imaginations,

Thereby banishing the prospects of insight,

Moral refinement and mental progress …

He would be yet another animal

A biped who knows not about his own intellect

His skills confined to survival and nothing more;

He is what he is through fine pruning

Through the endless churning of events

That remodel his thoughts and enable his psyche

To absorb the aftershocks of the happenings

That would bring him closer to the fields

Where the flowers of dreams thrive,

A consummative experience of life

That would nourish his soul …"

"The waves of randomness are unrelenting

Rocking the fragile boat and bringing forth panic

The caveman must have seen that dream

As he floated atop the canoe in a tranquil stream,

That everything is subject to change

And that there is an entity called time,

That would determine the happiness and sadness

And that he too would be a dead log of wood

Someday, when the light wouldn't wake him up anymore …

He was a long way away from the shores of language

Yet he had come to realise the core philosophy of life,

The beauty of transience and the flimsiness

Of his desires, though they kept him moored

Like others, to the pilings of earthly existence …

The fact was that he was not alone

In his sociable life in the thick of the woods,

But deep was the fear that was in fact alone

In his quest for the eternal truth,

That what is seen couldn't become unseen

That was the impression of permanence

Etched into the walls of his mind,

But the truth was starkly different,

Everything changes, diminishes, disappears

And not a trace of life is left behind

As if man himself didn't exist in reality,

He ought to be an ephemeral dream

In the mind of an ever-sleeping god,

What he saw in the darkness of the night

Maybe shreds of God's own imagination,

Everything was mysterious including himself

Though the mind yearned for lucidity

What he was left with in life was less than sane,

A reed basket of memories, with dew drops of poignance,

Life indeed imparted a feeling that was unique

And the feeling of one man was different to that of another,

Flowers in the same bunch do not share the same fragrance

The thoughts that maketh the man are distinctive

Though lives overlap, the idiosyncrasies don't,

Man was bound to be social in his circumstances

But he felt more like himself when in solitude…"

"The body does its allotted work regardless

Of time and the changes of the world,

It heals, scars, the cells take rebirth

Countless times without human awareness,

The garden has been in full bloom

Though it went untouched by the eyes

Due to the preoccupations of man,

What has been born strives to survive

To fulfil its earthily goal against the odds,

What perishes sprouts in the flower beds of memory?

Life is replaced by dreams even when extinct;

That brings into question the existence of the caveman

As a memory, though physically gone

He is there, stranded between a metaphor and reality,

As a prelude to life, a complex bodily form

With an infinitely complex mind that had thoughts

That gave another layer to the ephemera,

An intimate relationship with the concept of god

As a suckling seeking the breast milk of the cosmos,

A morally conscious being who found tangibility

In the sufferings of others around him;

He would not fit into the society of modernity

He may not have felt himself as adequate

For the tribe of his times as well,

He was an apostle of loneliness

One who found peace in the sanctuary?

Of his isolation from the rest of the world,

He who saw more with his eyes closed than open

One who could smell the fragrance of the blooms?

From a great distance, blurring the seams

Of reality with his rigorous meditations …"

The dusky veil with the embroidery of light

Shrouded the rock that stayed stoic

Though the mind was relentless in its verbosity

To exculpate myself from blasphemy

The monologue extended into the night,

Not as a diatribe against the illusionistic world

But as a contention for the hopes of the caveman

Who dared to dream of peace?

In an unforgiving terrain entrenched in violence …

A bird sang a melody as if learned by rote

A beetle trundled along the rocks as a routine,

The ants did their flag March with the dead lizard,

The night arrived with the radiant blue aura,

Countless stars gleamed through the veil of death,

In the boundless constellations

Lives perished and got replenished cyclically

Within the deep dark cosmic bowls of emptiness…

"Life's an independent body in itself,

Not tied into the acts of the motile mortals

It exists within itself, body and soul in one,

Where the physical and the spiritual cohabit

In the chaotic sphere of randomness,

Synonymous with the fertile nurturing earth

It exists not just here, but everywhere,

Even when it is invisible and imperceptible,

It is there in the conscious self

And in the deeper subconscious,

So febrile activities alone do not make "life "

One lives through the act of dreaming as well …

The caveman could only quote himself,

To be motivated he had to be perceptible

To the qualms within him, to seek and know

By exploring the deeper woods of darkness,

To him his life was the truth, precious but precarious

Time and again he would've the self-doubt

That he is changeable like the seasons

A transient phenomenon was life like the rains

Or lightning, the flesh revealed in a flash

Only to disappear and throw the man into despair;

He had the feeling of entanglement

Within the countless nebulae of time,

The unrelenting memories weighing heavily

Upon his mind, he was more like a plant

With its stalk bent towards the earth

Seeking the tearfully moist roots of existence …"

When one is sad, everything around him is melancholic

The bird doesn't sing anymore but wails painfully

The mind drifts from one season to another

Melancholy is but one continent of humanity

The joys are there on the other shores,

Though distance is bound to blind the views,

Man is no longer a subject but at the centre

Influencing the atmosphere as if by magic,

The sadness spreads like dark ink on paper

Placing a blot over the happiness

As if it never even existed in the first place,

The mind chooses what it wants to believe in

What it says with an air of authority, man obliges

The epicentre of imagination determines his life

To pick at random from the cornucopia of dreams …

"I've seen the lights at the temple

Dazzling, exuberant, visually stimulating,

They were celebrating the gods

Sending open messages to the cosmos

That they existed here, in the reality of time;

They believed this was their place

The planet of humans, the temple of the faithful,

The stars were auspicious, the gods danced

In the palaces within the cloudy gates,

Ensconced in the ephemera unaware,

Are the humans entranced by the lights?

Processing the spectacle with passion

As if it was a panacea for their ills,

The harbinger of the fortunes of time,

A bypass to the other world of colourful spirituality

Reflecting their devotion to the earthly desires,

But the happiness is unquestionably there

A period of cheers and forgetfulness of loss

The memories draped in optimism,

To be more imaginatively appealing…"

The tearful wetness of the autumn night is a reminder

Of the irrevocable ageing of mankind,

The body pines over the certitude of the passing years

Whilst the mind frets over its scruples

Unable to effectively dissect the fog of reality;

The duality of the existing man is a conundrum

What's true and (or) untrue, good and (or) evil,

Right, left, centre, periphery, directionless or not,

The ambiguity is pathognomonic of human existence,

Life isn't a straight line, but a series of lines

That creates several geometrical shapes,

Angular pathways and complex circuits

Through which the organism meanders

Drawing odd intriguing shapeless figures

As if sketching the outlines of extinct gods

To create befitting monuments,

As drops of rains adorn the surface of the parched earth …

"Sickness makes no one a saint

But the caveman had this strange vision

Of angels falling from the heavens

In robes of radiant white

When he became insufferably febrile,

The heavens existed in that space of delirium

As his constitution failed and the threat of death

Loomed large over the dreams of the man,

They held flowers in their slim hands

Soaked in the crimson of sunset,

Whether they were messengers of life or of death

He couldn't decipher, but the vision was clearer

As his senses began to detach themselves

From the giant leafy tree of life,

Were they angels or glowworms?

Imagination was at the height of its powers

When the course of time seemed to end

And the river was about to be set free

To become the sea …"

Liberating is the flow of words

Unobstructed by the self-doubts and anxieties,

God exists because of human art

And the enduring mystery of language,

Not just the fingers and the tongue

But life as a whole finds its meaning

Through the vocabulary of creativity,

The staggeringly complex circuitry of life

Is not solved by the uncanny knack of artistry

But it gives existence a newer dimension

That would permeate the barriers of fear

Throwing light on the incontrovertible truth…

"The caveman had his revelation

Through the random sequence of moments,

The lightning flashes, the thundering deluge

The sumptuous lives and their plight

Instigated in him the sparks of creativity;

Painful were his times, full of death and misery

The evolving intellect had to process the sights

Of the overwhelming natural phenomena

Through the teary eyes of the turbulent mind,

The shocks were succeeded by aftershocks,

He was aware of time, but knew not when it would end,

The dawn guaranteed a sunrise, but not human life,

He was the survivor of the night, having evaded death

Yet another time, but the game of chances was dreadful,

Surely life meant much more than mere survival

The flora appeared gallant, defying the floods

And the fauna continued their vibrant activities

Each of them seemingly with control over life

Though it was a culmination of fortuitous circumstances…"

"It was designed to be a mess

Chaotic, violent, incoherent, inane

Or was the perception being deceptive?

Everything happened as intended

Punctually to the dot, without a lapse,

The intention was that of a god or of many gods

The celestial formless entity that knew

Everything that needed to be known;

But the sun was one amongst many,

The universe perplexing in its expansiveness

Had no limits, at least to the senses of man,

This planet could be the nursery of lives

One amongst many in the multitude of universes,

For the moment, man was deemed to be alone

His life trivial and the world too sophisticated

But time would test the limits of his understanding

Was he not hearing the echoes from the other chambers?

On the other side of the cosmos,

Of lives, distinctive and replete with happenings

Of their own, as of mirroring the drama on earth?

Who were those souls who accompanied his ancestors?

Visiting him whilst asleep, as part of a dream?

They intended to speak to him, like the gods

But their language was untrammelled

By the prejudices of earthly vanity …"

They communed at night draped in the blues

Chanting ancient hymns of prescience

Awakening the soul within the man in slumber

To listen not with the ears but with the heart

To the words of collective human wisdom

That would lay the foundation of his esoteric inclinations;

The kites soared high in the clear summer skies

The children with invaluable joy held the strings,

They belonged to the future, but as an oneiric vision

He could see their scintillating eyes of hopes

The future beckoned them, from the wells of the past,

The world was pristine when man slept

Oblivious of the merciless trials that awaited him …"

It was sleepy and quiet like a pond

When the commotion commenced,

The new dawn brings in newer people

The crowds clamouring in every corner

Of the compartment, their vibrant incessant interactions

Transformed the isolated space into a society

Of people, their exchange of thoughts and worries

As if expressing solidarity for their own journey,

Strangers brought together by necessity,

Heading down the track set by the ancestors

Seeking the vitality of life in the wilderness

Disrupting the tranquility of the man

Who had chosen solitude as his abode…

"The cave gave the feeling of a hermitage

Though the man knew not who a hermit was,

Though he himself was the primordial one

Who had the moral seed of a saint?

He was impelled to give in to the voices

Of those around him, emoting and acting

His role as the man of a tribe, bravely protective

Willing to spill blood for the sake of honour,

He toned his behaviour to the requirements

Of the entrapping of civilisation

While deep inside he had the uneasy urge

Of questioning the established truths,

His existence too was natural phenomenon

Supposedly under the watch of the impervious gods,

He was bound to obediently toe the line,

Though the bloodless rebellion was active

In the silence of conformity …"

Like the nocturnal transformation of the landscape

The mind too changes its attire with the tides,

Imbued from the melancholic silence of blue

The thoughts changed colours like the surrounding leaves,

In the crypts of wild emptiness

Nature composed her most exquisite poetry …

"Who let the caveman into his room?

The dark den where bats took rest,

He must have had thoughts about his origins

Him being the progenitor of his children,

As the lives he had come to love perished

Nature seemed uncaring, flourishing

In the glorious golden sunshine

Which accentuated his sense of loneliness

Despite his deep rooted affection towards nature

That he adored as his mother, his only god

Who bore the seeds of his existence?

Yet when the room was dark and empty

And his fear about loss of love grew,

He would suspect the truth of his belief

In the benevolence of the mother

And that she too may be subjected to the whims

Of some other supreme being:

The fire of the universe

That cared not about the plight of humans

But existed regardless, as an entity

Rendering a masterly touch to the art of nature …

Blood flowed from one generation to another

Through the incessant art of procreation,

The universe too must have grown exponentially

As the god slept on his lotus bed…

The womb shed bloodied tears every lunar cycle

As an ode to life, that is lost and created again

The ritual of nature, praying to herself,

As the pilgrims in the cave transmigrated

Into the realm of an illusionary life,

Where salvation attained another layer of meaning

Biological existence overshadowing the truth

The light of the day had to be followed

With every life paying its obeisance,

The cave was the centre of conflicts

Between spurious desires and real challenges,

Where death was the only reality

And life reduced to a mere shadow,

With fleeting moments of joy embroidered

The intricate tapestry of deeper emotions …"

The cloud spreads across the night sky

As a bird stretching its tired wings,

The bedewed grass reminisces the day

Grazing over the memories of the herd;

The storm lamp watches over the seas

Fluctuant is the mood of the winds,

Many a lost sailor has been here

Uprooted from the world of his belonging …

"Every grain of sand is a seed of memory

Of lives that have walked the earth,

The cave is a living tomb of the past

Where the lone man vented his thoughts,

Looped into the experiences of trauma

Envisioning his future through dreams

Buried without having ever realised them …"

"i have woken up? Or is it only the muscular eye

That has palpated the first rays of sunlight?

The phenomenon of dreams has left me enamoured

With the memories of the art in that vast gallery

That exists in a dimensionless world;

I'm but a butterfly that has sojourned the space

Of the souls, where optics creates the finer illusions,

I've felt that I've been human all the way

Do the souls feel the same, that they do exist?

In real space, in real time, as living matter?

The dynasty that i have evolved from

Has many an "I", all of them individuals with genetics

The forefather believed that he alone existed

Unaware that he will exist through the lineage

Not as an individual or as the genetic seed

But as an idea, a fragment of intellect

That simply wouldn't succumb to time …

I am but one atom of humanity in a changing world

Within the incomprehensible universe,

I am yet unsure whether I'm a receptacle of things divine

Or i am the sole provider, holding the searching lamp

Unable to see through the chaos engulfing me

Though the roaring waves sound as if they are near …

I feel that I've emerged from the woods

Civilised, cleaner, equipped with urbanism

But the caveman tells me that I'm lying

I am bound to carry the baggage of the past

Accrued over the many generations,

i belong to as much to the present as to antiquity,

A prehistoric being that is rooted to the old soil

But has grown branches from which the bird

Can view the landscapes of the present times …"

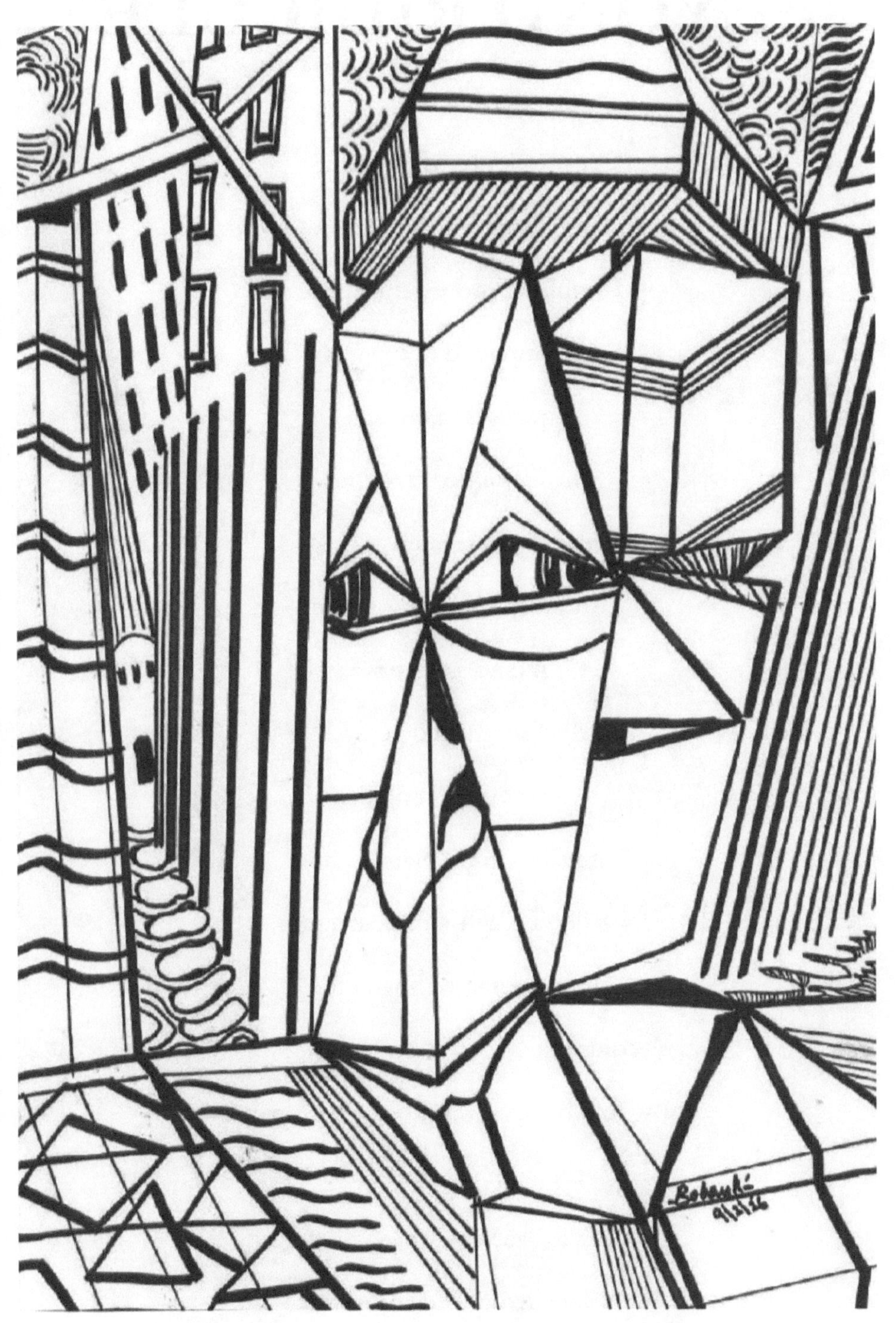

BEYOND RIDICULE

Yes… I'm becoming one

Amongst those around me,

I would become a metaphor

Of simplified humanity,

An equation that sums up

The disjointed fractions

Pretending to create an integer,

An independent molecule

Of memorised morals

And hardwired genes,

Assertively stating that

I am everything that I'm not!

I wouldn't laugh, but post a grin,

Tears would be shameful

A contradiction to super-manhood,

I would be presumptuously abrasive

I would be the archer

My tongue the strong bow

Firing arrows of rude words

At those daring to be my victims

Thus creating the aura,

The hyperbolic swag!

I would choose my visions

Not hearing what I don't want to hear,

I wouldn't tolerate any form of criticism

My wrath would be fiery torment

For those who threaten my ego!

I would see the street dog as a mongrel

A quadruped that deserves its fate,

Don't I relish the sight of those unfortunates?

Whom I regard as beneath me

Yes, of course I do!

Compassion is silly, kindness is weakness

And weakness is a threat to survival,

Life's a serious business

It's like a game of cards

The more astute one is the better it gets!

I would have my spirituality

As a strategy for my social stature,

Asset is my only goal

Not any fabled salvation,

I would claim that I believe in god

As I simply refuse to die!

I wouldn't leave the earth

For I am not a leaf, born to a tree

I'm a man, birthed from a womb

And have become

Painfully and rigorously

One amongst the other!…

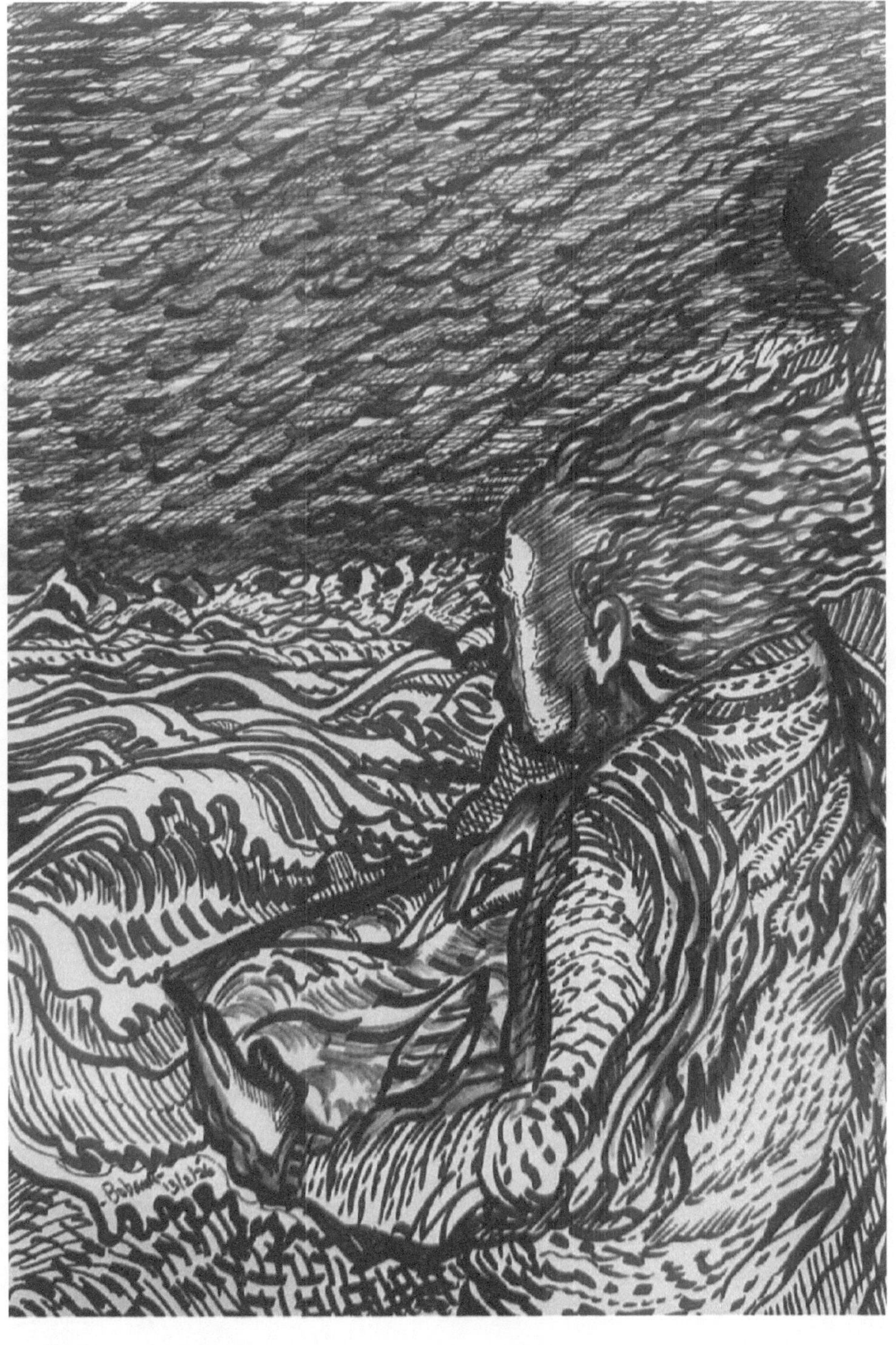

FREEDOM

Freedom is a good word

Uplifting, liberating

With wings of thoughts

Of emancipation

Of the intellect

And the spirit ...

One amongst the best of words

Gives the art of language

An unparalleled heft!

It is intensely exhilarating

As the paramount human idea,

But there's melancholy

At the deeper level of thought,

Sad indeed is the fact

That man needs freedom

Not from anything else

But from another man,

Or a human tribe

Or tribal dictums;

Freedom is a faith

An aspiration, the highest ideal

The pinnacle of human thought

The key to the evolution of man

And his sacrosanct concept of gods,

Freedom is beyond life and death

A monumental edifice of humanity,

As man struggles to construe

Why he who is born free

Is bound to die in miserable bondage,

Freedom in that sense

Belongs not the earth

But to the cosmos,

It belongs not to life

But to afterlife,

But is that true?

That which is tied in to gravity is (technically) unfree

One is unfree if he is attached to earthly things

But that would mean he isn't a mortal

A man is bound to love,

And love makes one free,

As he is blind to the consequences

The union of minds is freedom

That which brings forth new life

A newborn that is (philosophically) free

But the first cry is for the mother's ears

For her to exude the sweetest of milk

From her own heart,

So, the newborn too isn't free

Its mind a broad canvas

For thoughts to be painted on

With colours beyond its control,

For, humanity thrives in its complexity

Flowers of civilisation bloom in chaos,

Perhaps, man doesn't really wish to be free

He needs his earthly strings

The intertwining connections,

He loves as much as he abhors them,

Freedom is the loneliness of the heart

That feeling of uninvolved detachment

Within the cacophony of the crowd,

It is there in the art of the caveman

Who breathed life into the flat image?

Of the imposing muscular bison,

Freedom is tangible in its atomic form

But is too much to comprehend

For the intellect of man,

Conditioned to the algorithm of survival;

In the fathomless depths of human despair

Freedom abounds

As an energetic thought

An ideal for the mind to rise above the darkness

To empower the man continue his strife

To be really free …

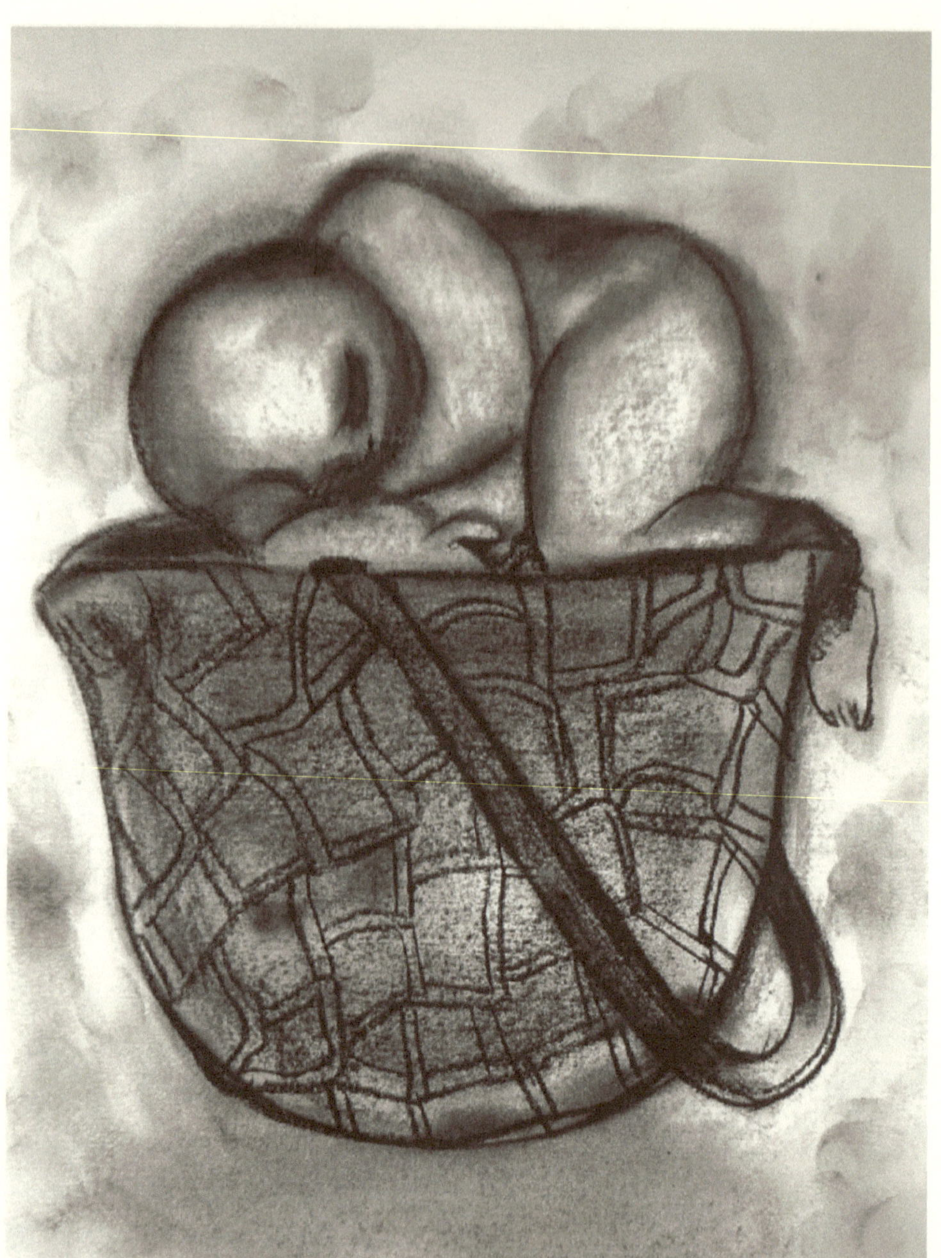

IN WARD X

It's a rainy morning,

The hospital ward is warm and dry

With finely striped carpets

The white lights aren't that hurtful

It's a Monday, yet there's a lull

As the patients watch random snippets

On their big phones, peacefully

Whilst nature is wet and singing…

The yellow flowers, a fresh beginning

The painting is soothing and lively

Like infants in their bassinets!

Anxiety is real, the blooms are there to quell…

The mind reassures all will be well

When the worries have found their outlets

For disease the treatment ought to be timely

Being mentally strong is the big thing!

The clouded grey skies are pouring

Down, making the plants appear comely

The meadow has newborn rivulets

Racing down the slope with childlike thrill!

It feels good near the window sill

Listening to the rains singing duets

Music enriches the mind's soliloquy

Life is indeed flourishing in every sapling!

The trees have donned another shading

Of dark green, making the imagination fly

Into the fantasies within the trinkets!

The mind is what brings light to the wooded dell …

Bitter to swallow is the white pill

But cozily warm are the blankets

Everything gets better by and by

The rainy morning, the yellow flowers, a new beginning!…

No one knows what the day would bring

The expectation is that it ends on a high

If only one could decipher the rain droplets

That tells man time doesn't stand still

The wanderer never reaches the idyll

In itself the ever changing time repeats

Creating a mirage of reality within a lie

The real and unreal are beads in the same string …

The patient next door is dreaming

In a fantasyland through his inner eye,

Like space shuttles are those seats

Which would levitate the inquisitive soul

The atmosphere is vibrant, yet it's tranquil

At heart, one patient drinks and eats

Whilst an older man lets out a faint sigh

Another patient is calm, his face beaming

About the future none has any inkling

It's as unpredictable as the sky

Living is the most important of all feats

It can't be learnt, futile is the drill

Life has to be lived out of own free will

The ward has a spectrum of inmates

Whose determination simply refuses to die?

Hope keeps one afloat even when sinking …

It's difficult for even those who are daring

When disease throws life into disarray

Even after the storm finally abates

The risk remains for thoughts to derail

Together the body and soul would sail

Till the point they've named as the fate

Man is wiser when he thinks his end is nigh

Wondering about the immortality death would bring …

The hospital is thoughts' eternal spring

Latching on to hopes that wouldn't go dry

He who is the fruit of destined gametes

Is outside, drenched in the storm of hail

He sees the other side of the tale

Through the window, his excited heart beats

As the pulsating umbilical cord would tie

Him to the moment of the newborn being …

That moment when the world was felt without seeing

When the novice knew only how to cry

Blindly searching for his mother's teats

The love for the air that would prompt him to inhale …

The patients try to offload the bale

Of worries, though they trust their wits

On the tools of medicine one has to rely

To help the body do the mending …

The desire for life ought to be unflinching

As time is not something one can buy

There's a wave of optimism as the bird tweets

And it softly echoes across the dale …

Every dawn arrives with a new mail

From the heavens, every time man breathes

It strengthens his inherent earthly tie

A natural act that doesn't need reminding …

It's good to be reborn, to feel like a suckling

That doesn't seek the "how" or "why"

What's necessary for life nature repletes

Herself with promptness without fail

Despite the melancholy, some patients regale

Themselves, refusing to call it quits

To survive in the world means to defy

The odds, though life itself is bewildering…

The volcano may be smouldering

Life could well be gone in a jiffy

The fire is hungry to swallow the peats

Of human life, and all the successes it entails …

On the same boat are the females and males

In the ward, confined to the drip stands at their seats

The registrar runs around like a spirited boy

With his bleep incessantly ringing

The boat is highly at risk of capsizing

No mortal can be sure of the ploy

Of fate, the eventful cycle in itself repeats

Through life and death, the gist of all human tales

What's on offer in life, man avails?

He's only alive as long as he breathes

Life is a mishmash of sadness and joy

Whatever happens, it needs enduring

One feels the melancholy in the passing

Of another, the feeling strong enough to destroy

His dream of invincibility, the flowers in the wreaths

Are lifeless, unlike the panting of water lilies

He doesn't know whether it's heads or tails

Life goes for a toss, what he sows he reaps

They say, but he feels more like a keyed toy

That has no say on its fate, mindlessly dancing

Like most in the world he is on the fringe

As the powerful set the rules, the lost guy

In a whirlpool of events awaits his release

Into a world of dreams set in surreal locales

There isn't a panacea for everything that ails

Humans, but man has the keys

To the doors of health, intricate is every buoy

That silently tells him that he needs medical testing

Without his awareness his body is rusting

Inside with age, he isn't made of alloy

The cells think and react to agents of disease

They work day and night not receiving a word of praise

There is the truth behind the haze

That life on earth is for a period of lease

The mirage of permanence is to decoy

Man, to make him yearn to be an eternal being

Man is sincere when he's dreaming

Of strange stories within his life's story

In that world he has nobody else to please

He's all by himself, to nothingness everything pales

There're signs conspicuous even in the nails

Of changing health, with age the risks increase

That nothing bad would happen is a folly

Of man, in the background the shadows are lingering

How he wishes he knew the art of undying

Lifting himself back to life! There's no alchemy

Or magical trick to help him seize

The youthfulness that never fades

After cycling through a few stages, life stales

The defiant batsman is alone at the crease

Anxious that the bowler would deploy

The fatal ball that could set his stumps flying!

The reality of the world is baffling

A mute spectator of events is the fly

Trapped in the web, the mind prays for peace

Knowing the truth is that there are no holy grails

When life's gone the body decays

Reality ends when the breath would cease

The eternal unseen soul that flies high

To the heavens is imagination's offspring

What's on earth is the sole sense of being

Nobody knows whether the rest is a lie

The countless lives that departed to the quays

Of eternity haven't come back to tell man their tales

On the seashores the children fill the pails

With sand, building the castles in their own ingenious ways

The moments fill the young hearts with joy

What's beyond sight is perhaps not worth seeing

The truth is embedded in the living

The reality of the world is a far cry

From the dream, yet it isn't all about death and disease

The breeze is true, so are the gales

But truth is bitter without the frills

Man tries to freeze his tranche of memories

Vainly hoping that it would never die

Eternity is a thought that's too compelling …

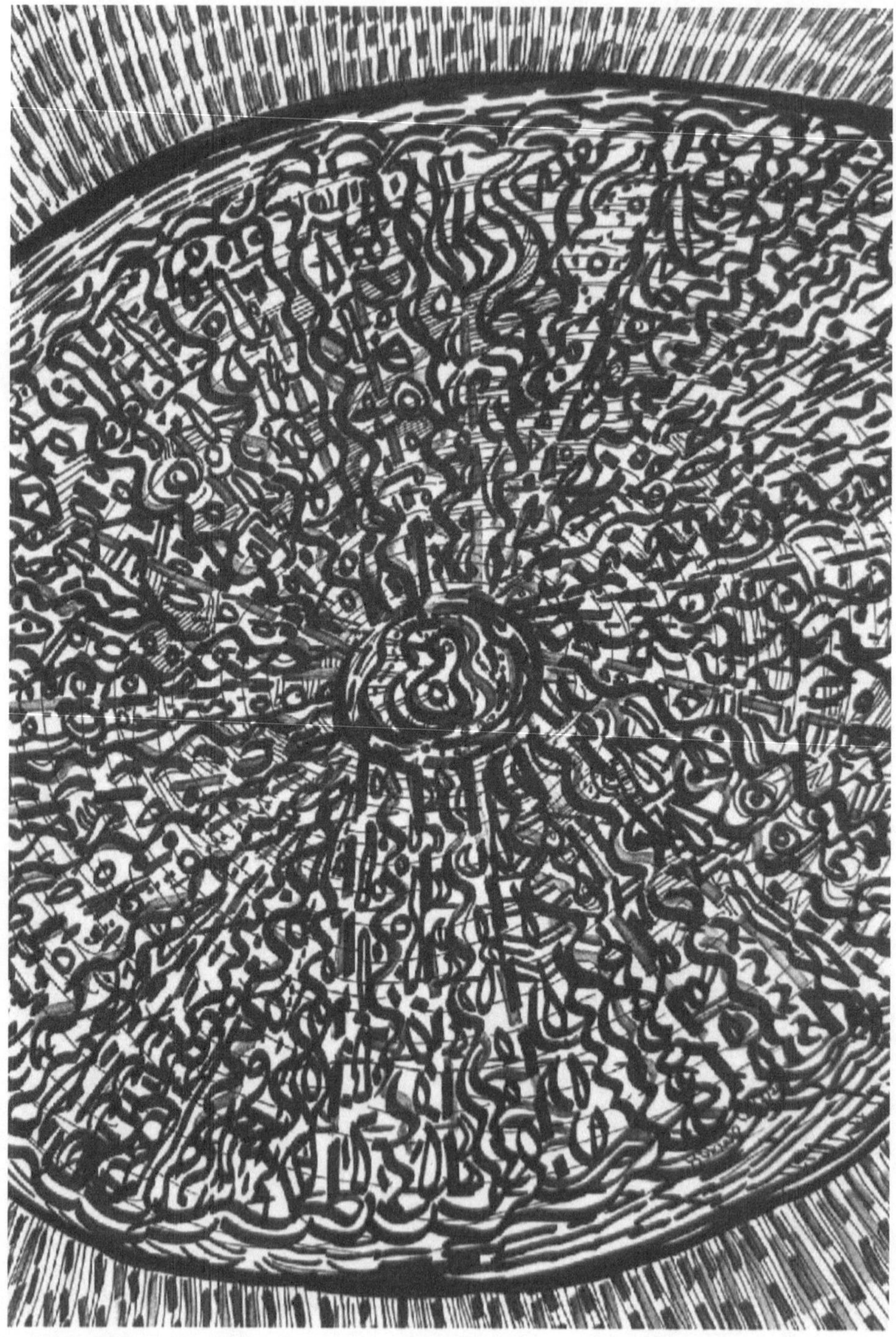

PAX

If light is wisdom

Then is darkness ignorance?

If the day is symbolic of life

Is the night equivalent to death?

Darkness is unassuming

A pure blank canvas

Giving life to dead stars,

The day is a derivative

With the pastiches of yesterdays

Vibrant with visible activities,

The night is the other side

When the mind finds its own space

Away from the turmoils,

It is true to heart, a mirror held to the soul

There is enough black ink in the skies

For the poet to pen his words,

The day is unforgiving, it drains the body

The night fills the mind with vigour

A spiritual quest replaces the mundanity,

The day leaves one empty and penniless

The night repletes the granary with its dreams

That would invigorate his journey,

Meditation attempts to create an artificial night

With the pearls of insight appearing as stars

Darkness, truly, is the guide to wisdom …

The day has many a character, all ephemeral,

The night has only one, the self

Figuring out its locus in the vastness of space,

The day is an inn, for feeding and fuelling,

The night symbolises home,

Reminding one of his cradle in mother's womb…

The day preaches through loudness

The night is contemplative, sublimely silent

Calm and restful is the harbinger of eternity …

Blissful indeed is the darkness …

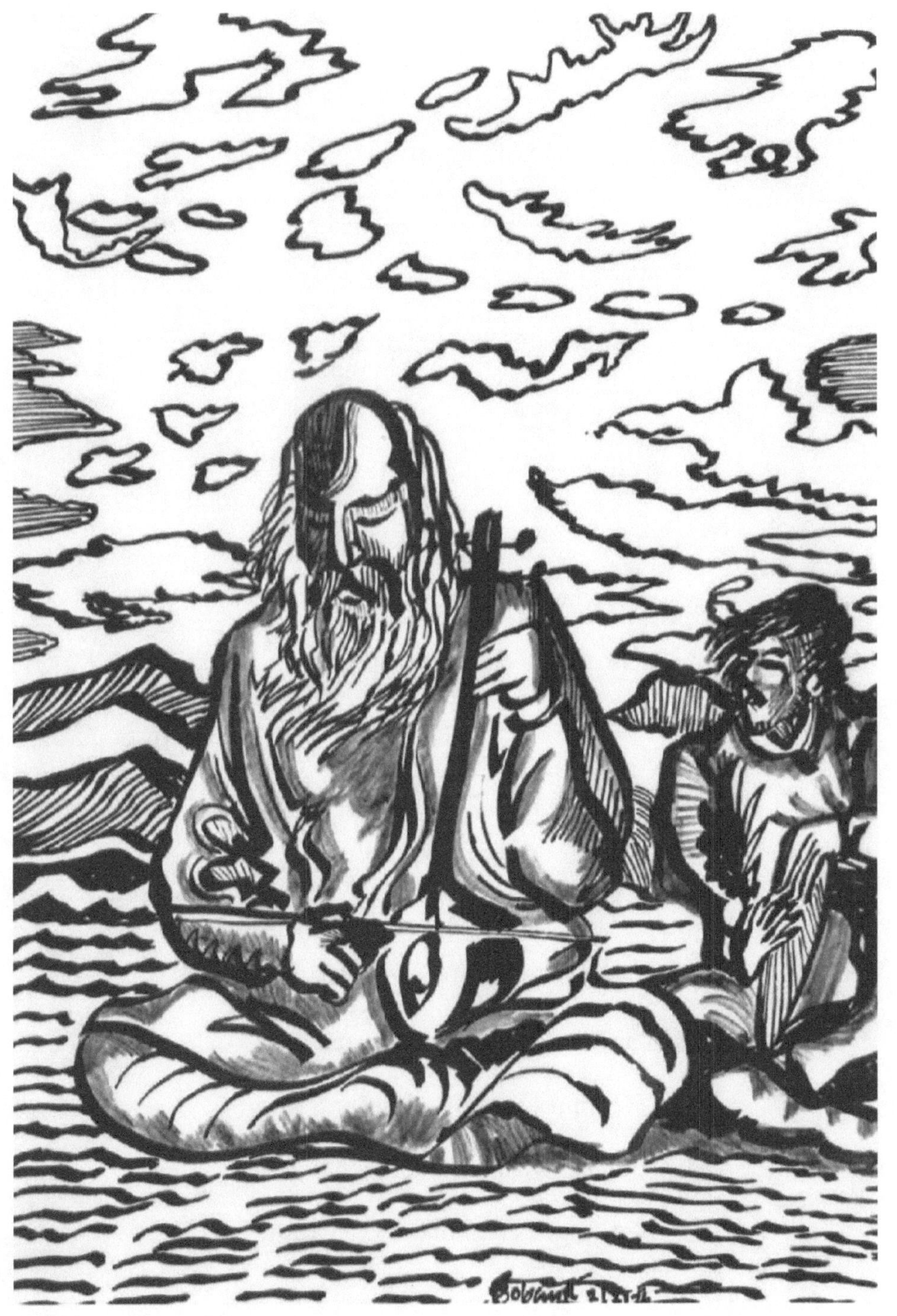

THE WAR

It is about six feet

Long, buried under the sleet

And rains, made of marble

An artistically etched scribble

On the headstone, on a clear day

In the blessed month of May

Reads quietly as follows:

"Here lies the man, wise and noble

Who attained the heaven's doors?

Like the man of the fable

His legacy lives on rock forever …"

It takes a stone to tell the tale

To the traveller at his encounter

With the tomb, in the dale,

This man was a good hearted one,

He thinks, there're flowers fresh

On the grave, long after he has gone

Not forgotten in the worldly rush,

Whilst the mighty king decayed into dust

With his buried gold that wouldn't rust

In the ever changing world of forgetfulness,

No-body even recalling His Highness,

This humble grave stands apart in silence

As the metaphor of afterlife

Nestled in the valley of bluebells,

A man who gained wisdom enough

During his life, passing it on to others

As the seasons fall like feathers

The self-effacing space retains a glow

With the peaceful impression of a dove …

The grass and the moss takeover

The bodily leftovers of earthly life

Man seeks success in every endeavour

Like immortality, which he knows is a lie!

All that would remain are some memories

And a bunch of flowers, they too would pass

Into oblivion, as universal is decease

But the vitality of life isn't a farce

Though short lived, it's the prelude,

To death which no man can elude,

The skies create a transfixing illusion

The winds have a musical percussion

Life is the summary of sensory experiences

Man wonders there could be something else

Beyond the grave, that's beyond matter

Between life and death, he trusts the latter

For deciphering the truth of eternity

And the unperturbed silence of the Almighty…

The thoughtful words that he spoke

Are not carved on the rock,

The true wisdom that comes with age

And that's isn't fearful of sacrilege

Is unfortunately lost to mankind,

The gist of the story that is left behind

Is a mix of wishful thoughts and moral tales?

That the soul must have met its allies

In the boulevards of paradise,

That which has attained the highest of heights

Is adored as earthly life is deemed fragile

Subjugated with ease by the gale

Of time, man trusts what happens after

His tenure, life at best could be called a satire

That mimics the ambitions of the gene

Ephemeral is the fascinatingly lively scene

That is inherently vulnerable to perishing,

Man is afraid, but pretends not to be a weakling

His vivid imagination artfully creating the netherworld

A spectacle for the souls to behold!

Doing no harm to others is the purest form of piety

Death comes to the rich and the mighty

As swiftly as the breeze shaking the cornfields,

Discharged from the confines of life and earth

The free soul enters the cosmos taking a rebirth

The distorted images begin to make sense

The earth has been one amongst the many inns

Where they assembled, quarrelled, partied and parted

Their hearts split between love and hatred,

The selfish cruelty and the inevitable chaos,

The vicious cycles of terrestrial wars

Are elements of the picture of humanity?

That is unwilling to admit its moral frailty …

Intellect doesn't enrich, thoughts frighten

The man, his freedom is relative and conditional

They would label him as a nation's citizen

Restraining him like a canine in a kennel!

It's as if only in death man finds his liberation

In the journey after leaving the way-station

The body doesn't mourn its own death

Like afterlife, earthly life too is a matter of faith

If the real world exists, it does,

Resplendent with the activities and gloss,

If it is deemed to be false, it is false

So there is no question of any loss!

The psyche seeks the meaning of attachments

To anchor the vagrant and to brave the torrents

Perhaps reality is but just one layer

Of an evolving truth, man is stuck in the quagmire

He ought to endure life and find his way

As lives and realities around him wither away…

In melancholic cold nights the poets would assemble

In the chamber of the ancient temple

Chalking out the intricacies of life through debates

One said: The earth is a prison, we're inmates

Desperate for freedom, beauty is just a distraction

To keep the mind rooted to the earthly station!

Another differed: the earth is the paradise

Perhaps the only one man would ever know

It is here that the one born lives and dies

There's no afterlife, nowhere else to go!…

Another joined in: our future we don't know for certain

For the morrow is veiled by an opaque curtain

We trust in God as an antidote to the poison

Of suspicion within, hoping the father would shield his son!…

Another voice: Man is essential diabolic

His morality is a bait for divine reward!

He is unaffected by the world being shambolic

As he believes that he is the God's own ward…

Yet another voice: do the extinct gods have an afterlife

Do the sculptures think and walk on their own?

They don't, man knows not how to deal with grief

And loss, hence the thoughts of the heavens he has sown!…

The master contemplated: the lowness of our mood has been lifted

By spending time in some verbal interactions

Without imagination, man is akin to being dead

He needs society and intellectual transactions

Whether this is a prison or heaven, it matters not

No man has found the magical oasis he has sought

By scribbling on scrolls, man liberates himself

The moon has come out shining, or rather her one half!

Light permeates the densest of darkness

For the grief stricken man, wisdom is the only redress …

Then they stayed in silence for a while

With the clouds standing still and the moon getting pale

The conversations ceased and they dispersed

Taking their thoughts with them to dream in bed …

The internal war demands proliferation

Of thoughts on the profoundness of life

It isn't a simple good versus evil equation

The tormented soul hangs onto the edge of the cliff

From where he vaguely sees the circles of hell

Where the countless incarcerated ghosts dwell

The earthly man struggles to silence his mind

Deeply disturbed by the war's atrocities

Dismembered bodies inside the rubbles in torched cities

Compel him to question his trust in mankind,

The nucleus of his thoughts is in being human

He knows deep inside that all are his brethren

The silence of the many comes back to haunt him

The light gets obliterated, the future looks grim …

Man is bound to fight the internal war

The greatest of all wars by far

He has inherited perceptions of good and evil

And has the choice of his own free will,

When he fights against many an inner demon

He doesn't have an army, he's utterly alone

Naturally he is confused, the darkness is confronting

The duality unravels his inner being,

Between goodness and badness, and the grey shades

Are the morals that have sharp blades?

That self-inflict the wounds tormenting him further

He is drawn deeper into a critical juncture

His experiences aren't helpful, his resources fail

Quickly has the breeze turned into a gale!

He wishes he could shut his eyes and fall into a slumber

So immersive that on waking he wouldn't remember

The quest he has ventured to undertake,

But peace isn't something that he could make

With himself, his heart is palpitating with anxiety

Gone is the wishful thinking for satiety

The mind echoing the thoughts of emptiness

Insufferable are the throes of existential stress,

The entire world collapses into the pond

The weightless body is like a water lilly

A colourless one that doesn't astound

Not a flower anymore that would laugh gayly …

The bodily cells strive to keep the engine going

Self-repairing and utilising the energy

Sustaining life, but what're the humans doing

To each other, slaughtering in a mad fury!

Hatred is the worst of diseases to endure

Fuelled by the burgeoning insanity of greed,

The mind sinks into despair, unsure

Wherefrom the wise humanity got the seed

Of self-destruction and fascination for death;

The body doesn't give up fighting till its last breath

Suffocated under the rubble, freedom brutally violated

A healthy life is pushed into the valley of death

They discard the corpse," a poor life ill fated"…

Life isn't allowed on earth to be lived in peace

Fate is a human construct that is dictated

By the powers who can't accept the world as it is,

Powerless in the endless cycles of madness

Is the struggling life, the fly in the spider web?

Unable to express its insufferable distress

The earth transformed into a devilish hub …

Fatal is the human fascination with death

Self-destructive is the sadism in inflicting pain on others

The brain fog is obstructing the true path

Deafening are the wailings of the bereaved

Mothers

That bruise the awakened conscience,

The broader humanity sinks into a stupor

Their own true voices held in abeyance

As precious lives are bombed into vapour …

There're no moral codes that bind humans

Except the voices of their own conscience

The debate is internal, and they take a humane stance

For that man ought to expel his own fiends …

The blooms of blood are fresh and warm

They simulate real flowers, thought without fragrance

Darkness quietly accompanies the storm

That ravages the garden with insane rants;

Life is defiant and puts up a resistance

Keeping hopes alive on the molten earth

Without the fire of hope there's no chance

Of survival, and blown out would be the last breath …

The smell of burnt blossoms fills the nares

Vainly attempting to cover up the stench

People go into hiding like scared hares,

It seems like life doesn't have any value as such

It is weighed up in gold and currency to create status

Money makes the mighty, the rest are weak

For them life is a battle, it is perilous

Caged in social stratum with locks they can't break …

Some say war is a projection of the internal conflict

Between good and evil, and the moral dilemmas

Man is the judge and he can declare the verdict

On his own deeds, he knows his civility is a farce

Within him is the demon that aspires for power

He has a taste for destruction and disorder

Falsehood is a useful weapon to deceive

And subjugate, peace is a meaningless reprieve!

The aspiration for truth to ultimately prevail

Is a dream, but for a world indulgent in chaos

The pretentious moral affinity is too thin a veil

That does not tackle the demon in-house …

The earth is much like the human body

The organs are ailing and under attack

In vainglory and ignorance they sing the rhapsody

Oblivious to the truth that the prognosis of bleak …

Man dreams of escaping into outer space

Having utterly destroyed his planet of birth!

He trusts the gadgets of his technological craze

To create colonies in other planets through stealth!

The endless greed would eventually destroy his clan

Playing god the powerful would chalk out a plan

To annihilate the rest and take the exit route

In their state of the art space-boat!

What one sees here in earth is all that he has got

But that falls on the deaf ears of the bigot,

Life is despised in the clamour for paradise

As humans become mere vectors of lies!

The calmness is foreboding, before the tragedy

Hate fuelled violence fills the human drama

For which love is not seen as a remedy

But as an abnormality, they nickname it as "karma "

When the future is really in human hands

And changes could be brought by collective action

Guiding the society in a positive direction,

But then, that's not what the demon within demands

Of man, there is the compulsion for retribution

And conquests, intellect is numbed by sensationalism

Gruesome violence becomes a thing of fashion

Ignored is the call to apply wisdom …

It's not that there is a dearth of the wise

But power resides at such tall heights

To those eyes common humans are invisible

The few who are seen are taken to be gullible,

The few govern the lives of all others

The few don't care even if the world is in tatters

Humans are subjects, of money and power

The mournings are not even faint murmurs

To their ears, men without guilt of remorse

Have no natural human sense of loss …

The skies are lit up by drones and not the moon,

People pray in bunkers hoping it would end soon

But sadly their future is not in their hands

They're puppets of men in faraway lands!

The insensitive have no problems sleeping

The compassionate one is a weakling

They say! Tribalism is what rules the roost

And in the din of vain pride humanity is lost…

The babies of tomorrow may despise their fathers

For seeding lives in a world in utter chaos

The foetuses in the deepest of sleep vividly dream

As the makers of future malignantly grin …

Peace drifts further away everyday

The isle of calmness isn't in sight anymore

As the tribes of humans wilfully slay

Each other, maddened by blood and gore

Is man who hates others of his brethren?

Bloodlust and greed obfuscate his vision,

The beast within man thrives in the chaos

Roaring with joy over the mounts of loss …

The sane minds foretell the catastrophe

But their voices are lost in the war cry,

Gratifying to the beast is the graphic violence

Numbed and muted is the natural common sense;

The displaced run hither tither seeking shelter

As the panicky sirens blow out the ear drums

The military operations are carried out to the letter

The devastated towns are turned into slums…

The conflict between men spans civilisations

Well before the birth of fenced nations

Wars have been futile, that's in hindsight

But the modern man is yet to see the light

Of truth, the focus isn't on human welfare

But on the flamboyant display of warfare!

The slain are all commoners, who have no say

Over the mighty, their dreams thrown into disarray

To endure squalor in the tents of refuge

Life becomes an inescapable cage

Where children are born into the darkness

Of a toxic future, they smile nevertheless

Enveloped by the fumes of falling lives

In the death knell of hatred, nothing survives

But the beast that can't be satiated

With the flesh and bones in the debris,

The unfortunate hapless beings are entrapped

In the ego clashes of powerful men and their hubris

Nothing wins in the end, except death

Though the shallow minds wouldn't accept the truth

They seek more wars, and more spending of weapons

On the injured, and rejoice as the sane world mourns

Over the loss of humanity, the gardens are burnt

And deep craters are dug on the ground

By bombs that bury the budding blooms,

They laugh spitefully, as catastrophe looms

Over humanity, driven to madness by greed

Even more hatred they would seed

Well aware that hatred is all that would be reaped

In the future, if such a thing even exists,

Nothing has been learnt from the blitz

War is a monster that masquerades as man's servant

It doesn't feel guilt, it doesn't repent

For, to the beast, peace is a cardinal sin

Even if death befalls own kith and kin

It advises its master that war is divine

As long as man doesn't realise he's insane

The mayhem continues, with irrevocable upheavals

And human lives shed like flower petals…

Beneath the soil are the stories of the dead

Who laid down their lives for the sake of wars?

Their groans unheard when they were wounded and bled

But the sites still bear the fragile scars,

Their lives were snatched away from them

By the warmongers who were at the helm

Denied were the simple joys of a life on earth

As the beast of war shook with mirth…

The longer one lives, the more surreal it gets

He learns that the deep cave is fathomless

And that the lights are not glowing insects

But flickering remnants of the fallen angels…

The power of insight doesn't embolden him

It is a double edged sword, he confronts

A real world that is heading towards doom

Destroyed is the foundation of human bonds

Hapless are the victims of manmade wars

The music is drowned in the whining of drones,

A bountiful habitable planet unlike the mars

Is slowly killed, darkness shrouds the morrows…

Wondering how much of this could be a dream

He strives to pick up on the cues of reality

The demonic humans are indulging in savagery

They've been devoured whole, the next could be him!

The panic stricken man is unwilling to succumb

To the pandemic of hatred, though his senses are numb

He puts up a struggle with his last resources

Knowing well that he would be overcome by the forces;

The minutes tick along, the sirens cry aloud

Over time the mind gets immune to the sound

More amplified are the palpitations of the heart

The adrenaline pumps keep the mind in high alert,

Man is an animal when it comes to his own survival

Hanging on to the vestiges of hope in the death knell …

The cells crumble unable to bear the stress

The eyes blurred by the smoke from the rubbles

The devil smiles masquerading as a human

Self-aggrandised by the death of the civilian,

Wiped out from the face of the earth are the souls

With none left behind to mourn over the loss …

Man becomes immune to death after a while

When like stacked logs of wood is the corpses' pile

Life's just another number in the maze of statistics

When bombs rip apart ancient societal fabrics,

The holes become craters and they become voids

Massive concealed graves for the bodies

About them history wouldn't talk, it avoids

The inconvenient truths, playing to the war lobbies,

Not a member of the global society, but a number

That is not worth an epitaph to remember;

They say the charred remains of the city are haunted

By the grieving souls, whilst the perpetrators sleep

In their cozy beds of riches unperturbed,

The butchers do not care about the slaughtered sheep…

Man is blinded with no insight into his crime

And he sadly lost all sense of shame,

The pummeling continues, the grim reaper would grin

As the displaced mourn over the bodies of their kin…

The orchard is buried under the ashes

The fruits aren't edible anymore, they're poisonous

The birds have been killed, the drone strikes

The yard is empty, there're no more mourners …

The musical instruments have been orphaned

As the old musician has lost his upper limbs

Under the heap of debris, is his hand

Yearning to play! Severed from the body, yet it thinks!…

The rains stay clear from the smoky clouds

Chemical vapours of gadgets of destruction

Fill the space, the jets flatten human abodes

The victims slain by the violent obsession

Of the strong are quickly forgotten

To perpetuate the viciousness of the cycle

Blood begets blood, going back to where it began

And it continues, though the mortal pain is a trifle

To the powerful who rule over the world,

The nursery is deserted, the birds do not sing

The missile takes off targeting the nestling…

The future is evolving, from nascent thoughts

And acts of humankind, it is part of the present

With elements of supine dreams born in the cots

The imagery renews itself into which man would transcend

Bringing him to the "future" in the time scale

There he sees familiar faces and forgotten dreams

In front of his eyes, his reality would fail

As a flood of imageries burst the seams!

The subconscious infers the innate fear

And the apprehension entailing the morrows

In the mist of self-doubt, everything is unclear

As wars rage between the tribes of friends and foes,

Lack of clarity of vision is what's ailing the man

He is partly dreaming, and partly living

He wonders what curse has befallen the human clan

The present and future seem to be the same thing…

Unpredictable like torrents are the human deeds

Repetitive are the stories of aggression and survival

Man behaves only in accordance with his selfish needs

Suspecting even his own shadow as his rival …

What lies beyond the frame that's visible?

He doesn't know, unrelenting is the sense of transience

Reality itself has the makings of a parable

The impressions are deciphered by his conscience…

On the one hand is the hegemony, the global order

On the other is the singularity of the human mind

That's invariably linked to the plight of others

Intricate is the web that binds together the entire humankind;

Nothing ever happens in the world in isolation

"The point in time" concept is a deception

Intertwined are the centuries and the tale

Of struggle and survival that man dreams all

The while!

He worries about the erosion of moral values

As the world meanders without a direction

If only man could think from another one's shoes, all that's required is
the compassion

To live and let live, for universal harmony

But the saga of mankind is one of vengeance

Driven by the insatiable greed for money,

Deliberately ignored is the essential common sense…

War kills, countless lives it would destroy

Poetic is the depiction of the battle of Troy

But in reality, like all wars it's bloody and violent

All wars are fought on a slice of land

For taking revenge or satiating ambitions

What ought to be spent on food goes to ammunitions

For upholding vain pride, creating ballads for posterity

Not a thought is spared for global prosperity

The demons within call for total annihilation

The egos are wounded, there is jubilation

Over the dead bodies of slain children

And they still call themselves human!

What was once fought with stones and spears?

Is now a battle of destructive machines?

The end of the world is nigh, man fears

There's no more scope for redemption for human sins …

The brute force pummels entire neighbourhoods

As the boots trample down the gardens

The peas won't wake up anymore from the pods

As they're crushed by so-called humans …

The spectacular war painting covers a wall

Like a rampart it is several feet tall

The horses are panicking, the fields are ablaze

The soldiers are killing each other in a craze!

Their upheld flags are of different colours

But all the wounded strangely look human

Their blood has been spilled over the moors

But the slaughter continues with elan…

The painting glorifies war, though it depicts the horror

The peasants aren't counted as if they're irrelevant

They would praise the valour in their folklore

Of their forefathers who defended their land…

The gory scene is recreated in modern age

The versatile actors are back on stage!

The firepower reduces bodies into ash

As the civilisations fatally clash

The plight of humans remains the same

As the injured and displaced seeking refuge

The machines hunt them like wild game

It's easy target, as they're within an open cage …

They say history repeats itself own mistakes

As history is made and written by humans

The blood of the innocent is flowing as lakes

As the world seems to move on without taking a glance …

The news brings cheers to the table

The breaking news of deaths of strangers

Like mindless puppets they babble

Some nonsense to appease the warmongers!

The powerful decide the destiny of others

Whether they should live, they aren't wrongdoers

But they're in the wrong place, the justifiers say

Lucky are those who live to see another day…

One's life is someone else's generosity

To the mighty peace is an act of piety

They crave for enough death and destruction

Before the word "peace" could enter their oration;

As long as the loss isn't personal, it is ignored

Though the slain is a human and his blood is red

They sense the otherness which gives them immunity

To guilt, alien to them is the human community

As they're immeasurably wealthy, the elite league

That has the authority to act rogue!

Uncertainty brings opportunity for business

Money is fished out of the deep mess

Ethics isn't an ideal anymore, morality is a farce

The world is torn apart by brutal force …

Sanity is a big deal in the world of absurdities

Where lives are traded as cheap commodities

The gods in heavens are unanimously silent,

The devilish acts on earth are rampant

Life is deemed worthless, to be pawned by the mighty

It has been the case since antiquity

That power is pure evil when absolute

That can buy loyalty and make the world go mute

When atrocities are committed as leisurely acts

Tearing apart the moral codes and peace pacts,

Man hopes for the realm of a higher justice

That would answer the victims' tears

They would realise the gravity of their crime

Their hearts tormented by guilt, in some distant time

But the lives can't be resurrected nor their dreams

Callously destroyed by a few men's whims …

Another great day for war, a sad for peace

Human lives are mowed over like flies

Enmity makes things easier, killing is allowed

To annihilate humans, they've avowed

The earth is destroyed with missile and machine

The pollution of the planet is not counted as a sin,

As chemicals impregnate the air and water

For them, nature is just another laughing matter!

They turn the world upside down, to self-aggrandise

Forgotten are the enduring words of the wise

That truth is not borne out of a pack of lies

And that peace is not borne out of war

Nothing is learnt from history, but painful is every scar

Left on mankind by the enforced death and displacement

Alas! For the shut eyes there is no room for enlightenment …

Is there a magnetism to the "art" of war?

That paralyses the senses and enthrals the mind?

Lessons learnt from history are so rare

As if war is a psychotic affliction of mankind…

Goya painted the devil in his nightmare

Vague form, sinister in appearance

Mortifying is that cold impassive stare

Like a beast calmly waiting for its chance

To prey upon the unsuspecting humans,

The artist's deafness shut him out of the world

He could see clearly through the mist of trance

That on the warring earth, the devil prowled

It was only a matter of time before it all ended

As a civilisational disaster, as men devoured each other

Not out of hunger, but to satiate their anger

The artist saw that in a world where morals are dead

The future was bleak, the voice of sanity in vain

Would remind humans indulging in violent fantasies

That the end is nigh, and nothing would remain

If they couldn't get over their worst disease:

Greed, and the mayhem that it would instigate

Through vicious cycles of death and destruction,

If instead of natural love they resort to hate

The end result is inevitable self-annihilation…

The excited news anchors blare their horns

The experts sell their disastrous predictions

Whilst in a distant land a poor mother mourns

Over the loss of her child, her heart bleeding from the gashes …

The real mannerism ought to be humanity

That bonds every single one of humans,

Peace the only route to maintain the sanity

Chaos is what results from the conquests of lands;

Instead of accepting the truth with an open heart

The human primates throw fireballs at each other

The powerful ones try to act street smart

Pushing the weaker ones to the end of their tether!

The story tellers seek tales of blood

Unsensational are the news of something good

Blatant lies are peddled as sacrosanct truths

Incessantly vociferous are their warmongering mouths!…

The descend into mass chaos is a real possibility

As the bloodlust seeks even stronger violence

Humanity is absent in the minds of the tyrants

Evil has a reputation for its banality …

Too many war is psychologically unacceptable

But they are lead to think it is inevitable,

The victims of the disaster have no choice

But to flee their homeland, burying their joys …

The dark quiet room is the safest place

Where invisible angels sing sweet melodies

Enticing and inviting the man into the maze

Of sleep, the true panacea for his disease

Of fear, of bombardment and peril,

The vehicle of dreams would transport him

To a world none indulging in the kill

But has hearts of love full to the brim,

He can forget the blood stained walls

Of the classroom and the voices of children

Silenced, unable to answer their roll calls

Slaughtered like hapless calves in a pen,

The relief is temporary, as truth stays on

Indelibly scarring the heart, all is well

Till he wakes up after the night has gone

As it painfully sinks in that he's in a living hell …

Piety without love for humanity is futile

There's no room for god in a violent world,

They know it, yet they tend to believe in a lie

That truth is simply a false story retold,

The present has uncanny similarity with the past

The future is born from the seeds of the day

Haunted by the ghosts of lives lost

The peace on earth thrown into disarray…

The powerful don't dream, for they don't sleep

As they're petrified of seeing nightmares

They've plenty of wicked secrets to keep

Safe in their heavily shielded lairs!

Any measure of sanity is too much to ask for

In a challenging world that despises truth

From the isles of peace, mankind has drifted too far

With open hatred, they wish each other swift death…

Life could have been something else

Peaceful, through kindness and understanding

Sadly man is prone to be influenced by the spells

Of violence and the bloodshed from the killing;

It could be the protracted infancy of humankind

Still evolving, unfree from the shackles of violence

Millennia of history has been left behind

Yet, to man, peace doesn't make any sense!

With sadistic pleasure, the mighty orchestrate wars

To appease their insatiable territorial desires

They calculate deaths behind closed doors

With no plans at hand to dowse the fires …

There's no permanent solution to the malady

Of hatred, the scourge of humanity

To the warmongers, war entails collateral damage

Meaning civilians are bound to die in a cage …

The bodies of soldiers are flown home

Draped in the flag, to be saluted and buried

Forgotten by many, remembered by some,

Youth killed simply because the powerful wouldn't heed

The horrors of the past and the painful lessons

Leaving the mothers to mourn over their sons …

War is great, mass death is simple statistics

The rhapsodies proclaim the valour and pride

Ill-fated and ill-timed were those who sadly died

That's the tone of those who laud the violent invasive picnics!

Human minds are attuned to acceptance

The ones who hold power have the authority

The enslaved are impotent in taking a stance

Believing that the last word is that of the

Mighty;

Fire is rained from the skies over the hapless

Life is discarded as trash, morals are extinct

The conscience rebels, but the world is voiceless

They say violence is a basic human instinct

Even if the situation isn't dire or perilous,

Violence is entertainment that's is synced

Into the psyche, though it appears delirious!

That's the justification for the muted response

To the pain and suffering of the victims,

They're helpless preys to the fanciful whims

Of the powerful ones riding the high horse,

The suffering of a man isn't the pain of another

(For) they're not bonded by blood or clan

Even the wailings of a bereaved mother

Fall on deaf ears, immune has become man

Not just to many an infectious disease

But to the natural sensitivity to human plight

Seeing the carnage they're still at ease

Death is just another momentary news byte!

By virtue of birth some have been saved

From the premature death in war torn lands

They say the unseen destiny has favoured

Them, lest they would've been trampled over like ants…

The unlucky ones are entrapped in the cycle

Of hate and violence, with no end in sight

The phase of peace is sporadic, but fickle

Life isn't guaranteed as a birthright

The callous world fails them miserably

Deliberately ignored are their pleas

There are no issues that can't be settled amicably

But only if they worked towards universal peace …

The angst is exhausting, it takes its toll

The weary one falls into a deep sea

He can no longer hear the insane brawl

Sleep-time is when one is finally free…

He does the crossing, it's a whole new land

Where there's the harmony of yesterdays

His boisterous friends are performing as a band

A cache of memories that time couldn't erase!

The buildings are unscathed by bombs

There are lives teeming, poetical is the air

Peaceful are the people, there are no mobs

The boys sing and dance with much flair;

The newly born one can breathe peacefully

The war was a nightmare, it has ended

It feels so surreal, a dreamer's folly

Is what the mind thinks, he must've landed

In a fantasy world, with wishful thoughts

But the real and unreal are tied by knots

So tightly that it is difficult to distinguish

Between them, in the sea he is a fish

Not of a shoal but in a world of his own

He appreciates the people, yet he's alone

Swimming past the wreckage of warplanes

And the bodies blown up by land mines;

He sees them, how come they're ignored

People have been seduced by the rhetoric of the warlord!

There is an unmistakable undercurrent of poignance

Even within the allures of a paradise,

The blood stains on the school walls painted over

To conceal the deeds of human beings

At the end of the war, everyone is a peace lover

Even the mongers of wars become angels with wings!

Peace seems unreal, he certainly must be dreaming

The quietude is strange, the airplanes aren't humming

The death tunes, the rubbles have been resurrected

Into fanciful structures, the monuments of the dead …

No more pains of war to put people asunder

The babies can sleep in bed, not in bomb shelter

"Peace "has been written with the blood of innocents

All is going to be well behind the constraints of the fence …

It's a rabbit hole, but he is enchanted by the maze

Like the dream he hopes that peace stays

Let the tiredness of war make people sober

And let the warlords go into a deep slumber!

The prayers in a dream have no sanction of the conscious

No more smoke choking the lives, no more fires,

Yet who would hear the prayer in dreams

As man sleeps in his world, god sleeps in his …

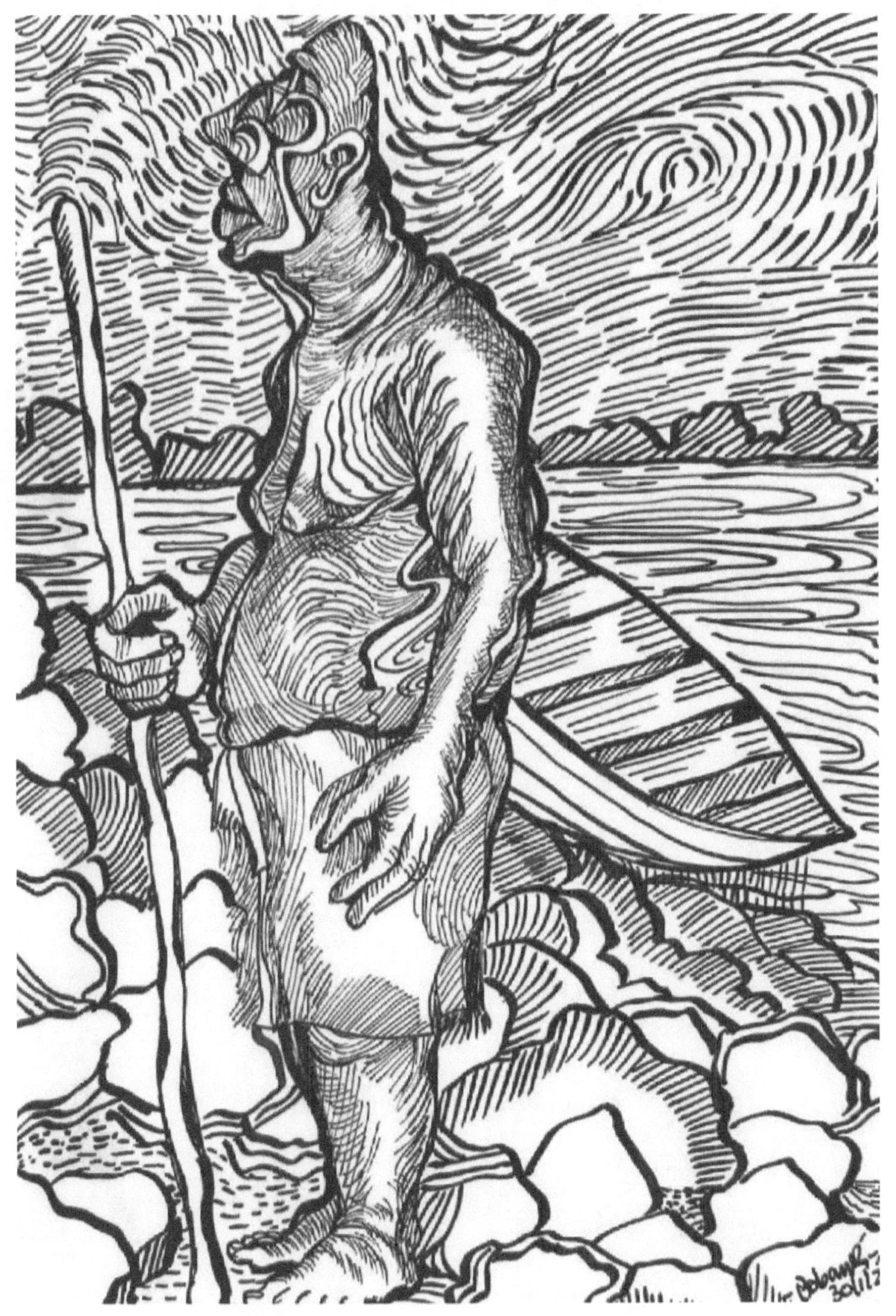

TRAVELOGUE

A busy place is the port

Where folks flock together

To cruise in the air-boat

Hoping to reach lands farther …

The sleep deprived eyes

Crave for the lost dream,

As they climb the heights

Where the dawn would gleam …

The sinking would be swift

Into the cave of deep slumber,

Whilst the mind would be adrift

In the early frost of December …

The ribboned clouds titillate

With their colours and hue,

A dream is drawn on the slate

Where life is reborn anew…

The sky is one unending path

Through which many had journeyed

Man believes the gods of myth

Reside there to judge his earthly deed…

The machine barely makes any sounds

As sleep disarms the stream of thoughts,

Densely impermeable become the clouds

As men fall into the rose scented cots…

The trees are heavily laden with blooms

Like the sleep bags under the eyes,

Fascinating is the cloud as it plumes

Painting lavishly over the cotton skies …

In the skies man is not even a minion

The earth the tear drop of a star,

The child is active with the crayon

Bedecking the dream with images from afar…

The firmament reminds that life's nebulous

Reformed by the experiences of moments,

The illusions are transient and superfluous

But the beauty of the dream is the transience …

The fog magnifies the mystery of being

On a planet that is perceived to be alone,

But the gist of life is in believing

That the passing illusions are one's own …

The earth is said to be a transit point

Where people gather to be warm and fed,

Not knowing whether they would be rejoined

With the place again they go to bed …

They fly over the tightly bounded territories

States and nations with their bloodied history,

Man claims command over the lands and seas

Only to self aggrandise with vainglory!

The boundaries exist till the end of life

And then no more, death doesn't debate with vanity!

Would man ever know his life was a lie?

When he's no longer matter, but a point in infinity?…

The most is chaos, the rest left to a dream

What's life but a collage of memories?

Man is no wiser when his lungs run out of steam

Succumbing to death, for existence to cease…

Even if time adeptly keeps repeating itself

Entrapping everyone in an illusionistic capsule

It is relieving if man could hang on to the belief

That he isn't cognisant of him pretending to be a fool!…

He needs to adhere to the stubbornness,

His inborn instinct to be like the invisible,

The fetus is immortal but dies in uterine wilderness

Unable to pass through the biological cribble…

Within the shell of the giant aircraft

Carefully driven by human strangers

Many a soul takes the much wanted rest,

Hypnotised by insufferable tiredness…

Many a life resides within one cubicle

Of flesh, bones, nerves and blood,

One life is a singular plight of a particle

That has only got the logic of a cloud …

Man sees in the embers in the ashes

The sanguine eyes of an immortal soul,

That is his palliation for the gashes

In a journey headed for a black hole …

The leap into the darkness is spontaneous

Not an iota of concern for the years spent

On earth, the eviction is instantaneous

In such a haste is the hapless tenant!…

There's no wonder that man has faith

In the invisibles and the omniscient divinity

He is journeying through the ancestral path

Littered with coincidences, hoping for an epiphany …

The world of the present is transient

The future could be a fantastic imagination,

Ephemeral is everything that's apparent,

Within the solidness is the potentially fatal fibrillation…

The bird knows not just the nocturnal songs

But talks to itself on spring days in soft whispers,

Perhaps the soul knows to where it belongs

After emancipating itself from the embers …

The night is fervent within the cave of silence

When time recedes into insignificance,

Ensconced within the illusion of a trance

Is a new world with its brightness immense…

The many scars are ossified inside

Trauma in itself is one stubborn memory

Man seeks a place desperately to hide

But illusion is the hope of such a territory…

The soul of Dorian Gray is aged

As it is corrupted by every human sin

The portrait of the mind that's deranged

Reflect the demon that's thriving within!…

The dollhouse is entranced in the serenade

As the phantasms of gothic tales waltz,

The notes crescendo and then slowly fade

As the velvet curtain of autumn night falls …

There are incantations in the hall of silence

So faint that they're imperceptible the humans,

There are things beyond the disciplines

That can't be perceived by the earthly sense…

The jaundiced lights enliven the space

Into which the man enters at night,

The mice squeak from the twisted staircase

A sense of adventure baits him from the height …

At times wails can't be told apart from laughter

When the mind is muddled with fatigue,

But any roof is home for the miserable drifter

Who is captivated by the mounting intrigue!…

There must have been inhabitants there before

The walls subtly speak of human bonds,

But every room is empty behind every door

The stillness is punctuated by strange sounds…

Past the vacuous spaces is the door to darkness

The space where a shadow is tied to the giant sundial

Incarcerated forever in the emptiness

As the newcomer enters, for a moment the time stands still…

Could a man ever be perfected?

His freeness of well in the heights of freedom

Where he is no longer afflicted

By the anxieties of the future yet to come?

Could there ever be a being as Siddhartha

Who could extricate himself from the woods?

Of worldly desires, the illusion of artha,

No longer affected by the meaningless goods?

The highest point of detachment

With perfect control over the senses

Would be like the bird of the firmament

That has nothing to do with the manmade fences…

Too hungry to feel any hunger

Too thirsty to feel any thirst,

Equipoised towards human anger

And no longer poisoned by lust -

The commander of the disarmed army

Of senses, in absolute control,

Unconcerned about fame or infamy

Has not mere existence as his goal …

The poetry of the ever changing nature

The tales untold by death and decay,

Speak volumes about the caricature

Of life, unreal and that would certainly pass away…

The selfish salvation of the unseen soul,

A misconstrued constricted version of spirituality

Reduces life to something mean and foul

That is over-simplistic in its thoughts on immortality …

There's probably none to judge the deeds

Of a fallible naturally imperfect being,

Thus quoth Siddhartha to himself listening to the reeds

Playing to the music that was deep and moving …

Man is more affected by sorrow than by happiness

As there's the gravity of loss in the former,

The beauty of life is masked by the senselessness

Of the senses, creating dark melancholy in summer …

Those who have left the shores do not return

Their memories scorch the living hearts,

Insufferable pain is what tends to govern

The living, with life being visible only in parts …

The illusion of fog shrouds life, which itself

Is another illusion, stubborn and poignant,

The wanderer doesn't know his own self

Unaware of its own stature is the elephant!

The smog is a perpetual hindrance

Maybe, it too has a purpose as a sign,

Of the consequences of human negligence

That the distraught nature would no longer be benign…

The urbanites meander along half blinded

Even the immediate vicinity is impermeable,

The traffic is heavy, the snail-pace seems dead

The streets are tired as the engines incessantly rumble …

Imposing are the structures of bricks and mortar

Ambitious is the dream, the city unabashedly keeps expanding

But the urban dweller is no superhuman avatar

He needs clean air to remain as a living being…

The crematorium is busy with the chambers at work

Dismantling the bodies into the elements,

The characters have completed the arc

They ought to go, having lived their allocated moments …

The megalopolis doesn't pause to think

As thinking is deemed to be a futile exercise

In a world that has been brought to the brink of extinction,

But they continue to believe their own lies…

In the warm cot of the mother-baby unit

The tender rosy cheeked newborns share their space,

They yet don't have a memory to forget

As they wait to suckle in the maternal embrace …

Tossing and turning in bed is the wealthy man

Whilst lost in an enviable deep sleep is the tiller,

At night, most are equal, slow and wan

Rampant but under diagnosed is insomnia, the silent killer …

The kites hover above the carcasses

Of concrete giants in the urban world,

The street urchins confront the bulldozers

About to pummel the castles of mud …

Life thrives on the makeshift cricket ground

With lean figures in various poses of motion,

Though under mounts of dust their world is drowned

Every living moment is a cause for celebration!…

One cannot see the silhouette of clouds

In the skies painted in a deep cold white,

The faithful strive to know the divine whereabouts

By praying in front of the holy lamp light…

The figures appear to have been thawed

After a long freeze in some volcanic eruption,

There stands the ancient city by the yamuna, that bestowed

On the world the jewel of human civilisation …

The lives are fluttering around frenetically

In an effort to survive the adverse tides,

They are neglected as the unsightly underbelly

Hidden by the shrewd tourist guides …

The poetic quest begins with nature

Striving to realise the nectar of life,

Through minted words he tries to capture

The cryptic codes within loss and grief …

Mary Patty died alone, unsung and infirm

The talented artist of many a humanist caricature,

She who wouldn't compromise or conform

To the norms, herself became a forgotten miniature…

But the artist restlessly engaged in a dialogue

With the mysteries of the existing world,

That's legacy enough for the body in the morgue

Art survives on its own, it doesn't need a tomb of gold …

The ascent to the heavens is treacherously difficult

Beguiling is the hell on earth or elsewhere,

Man is entrapped in the belief in the occult

Sinking slowly and irrevocably into the quagmire…

The benumbed faculties seek easy answers

To the most perplexing questions of mankind

The trust is placed on the crafty soothsayers

Whilst turning a blind eye to the voices of mind …

Is the journey half way through, or more?

What lies beyond this veil of surreal placidity?

He thinks, anxious about what's in store

That's what has vexed man since antiquity…

The night is the magnified shadow of the day

It has always been there, unspotted by gullibility

It's time for newer characters to enter the foray

To thrive before being consumed by their own fallibility …

The dream is centred on the beauty of friendship

Of the few who share their inner thoughts,

The book of life indeed has no divine authorship
It is nothing but the creativity of human beings …

At the crossroads, the thoughts diverge
Into the bypaths blanketed by dandelions,
Images dart like stars across the gorge
Which the child within captures with his crayons!…

The images step out of their frame
Into the empty room with creaky wooden floor
The night remains silent all the same
As a cool breeze visits through the half open door …

The collective impression is sublime yet puissant
Upon the mind that finds sanctity in the surreal,
The distorted imageries seem to be distant
More fleshy than the fruit itself is the orange peel…

The art of the imagination is silent
The sounds subtle, the presence invisible
It is never loud, nor is it ebullient
Yet it creates an illusion that wouldn't crumble!

The travel of thoughts isn't announced

By pompous trumpets as a parade,

It is silently eloquent and profound

Poignantly sublime like a serenade…

What would man do without his imagination?

His life depends on his power of dreaming,

He weaves stories with love and passion

His future is of his own making!…

The statue tells a tale of melancholia

As the languid night listens patiently,

Quietly floats the face of ophelia

With the eternal grace of a butterfly…

What prevents stagnation is the flow

Gentle and unhurried along the plains,

Transient is the joy, so is the sorrow,

Equipoised, the river doesn't flood with the rains …

The visual is one amongst the many

Of the imprints from the existing prototypes,

But the inner vision of the mind is uncanny

In its liaison with the phantasmagoria of dreams …

The world of atoms is fervently mobile

Colliding and creating with unbridled energy,

From the meditative stoic to the invisible reptile

Life and death flourish with ineffable synergy…

The leaves have cast away their shells

The oysters within dissipated into vapour,

Does the soul hear the heavenly bells?

Or like the body would it be in perpetual stupor?…

The frog owns the entire pond as its well

Sacred to profane, elation to mundanity

Everything is transitory within that cell

Of the body of the world, like the world of humanity…

What's man without his accouterments?

Of sycophancy and egotistic silliness?

Yet he has recorded on the parchments

With pain and agony about his existential weariness …

In the heart of the universe silence abounds

The blue lotus at night exudes a mystic charm,

What's really happiness without any bounds?

What's the shape of the soul without the human form?…

The stellar night speaks of deadness,

The cold reflection of afterlife from the cosmic rocks,

But the impression thrives in the stubbornness

The illusion of a ship sailing the seas, but still moored at the docks…

The dream is vivid, filling the voids

Of lifelessness in the deep wells of the night,

The mermaid bedecked with luminescent seaweeds

Swims ashore in the crimson cover of the twilight …

The world is the pleasure of the eyes,

A concoction of many a conflicting visual,

Only through reasoning at its heights

Can the sensible be winnowed from the sensual…

Delight is an essential component

Of the result of multi-sensory processing,

In the visual chaos man sees his opponent

That reduces him to a senseless thing …

When the twilight blooms like fresh rose

Like a new dawn, apparently the same,

The body with its innate clock seeks its shelter

It's fascinating how perception narrows the chasm of time…

Within the frame of physical time and space

Stands tall the peculiar portrait of man,

Who has his own mind, his mortal face

Radiant with the thoughts of a divine plan…

Freedom of will is a perturbing thought

For the man who fears the power of reason,

It is a blade that is too sharp, rocking the boat

Of sweet simplistic complacency with derision!…

Thinking is the originator of pain,

The unrest sows seeds for the chaos

Without that upheaval life would be in vain

Flooded and doomed like the mill on the floss…

The stoic would sleep on the sea shore

Caressed by the morning waves of summer,

Not for him the vainglory of blood and gore

Or the stellar but transient larger than life glamour …

Where exactly is the free will of a monk

Who finds salvation through renunciation?

There is a chant in the striking of the gong

The beauty of life is unearthed through contemplation …

Knowledge is gained through studies

Wisdom is ingrained in the mystery of life,

In the burrows of time are the keys

To unlock the meaning of loss and grief …

Man ought to educate his offspring,

Tend to them with care to help them grow,

The bird doesn't teach its child how to sing

The infancy of man is protracted, the track is slow …

One day he will be ejected from the dream

With a parachute to land in the unknown,

At a distance a lone star would gleam

A new sun, a cusp of a new dawn!…

The shades of emotions are pervasive, though with gold

Are gilded the screensavers of compassion,

The world of others transmigrates into the man's world

Where he stands to lose his unique distinction …

He cannot but be sociable in the din

Whether he likes it or not ,he ought to hide his own self

For fastidious trueness of self is regarded as a sin

Between his trueness and likeness he need maintain a sane gulf…

People crowd together to amuse themselves

Whilst the soul rests on the tree

Of salvation amidst the fluorescent leaves

The long sleep is when man is truly free…

How populous is the dream!

A few visible, most are shadows,

The suppressed desires of man let off the steam

The shores are vibrant, as the mystic river quietly flows…

The room is confined to the walls

The soul isn't; the loft is still accessible

With the cob webbed cluttered faces of dolls,

Man tells himself that past is indelible…

The wax melts and the walls peel off

The face of the dream, to become other things,

The hand patiently kneads the dough

To bake other figures, dreamy siblings!…

The skies appear to be devoid of birds

As the dawn approaches the harbour of the night

Wakeful are the light sleepers in the herds

Whilst the shepherd floats in the dream like a kite…

There will soon be the footsteps, of people

And their baggage of worries,

A rain drop descends and forms a ripple

As the train passes into another station of stories…

The actors do not belong to the theatre

They're bound to act, that's their purpose

The emoting, the jest, the operatic tenor

Delivering with precision the abstract poetry and prose…

The ferryman departs, to other islands

The oar piercing the sea of silence,

The footprints rest peacefully on the sands

In a long night's dream, blissfully intense …

The shells of the lives cast away

Become nests for the weedy moss,

Yet other lives would come to stay

In the fathomless repositories of loss …

Is the cycle of life thus unbroken?

Stretching from unknown to unknowable?

Knowledge is a misnomer for the ignorance of man

His shroud of sanity is questionable …

Everything would stay, he hopes with earnestness

But nothing does, that's the veritable truth;

Reality scorches him, yet he dreams nevertheless

Illusive is the butterfly, so is the moth …

The pendulum moves, the time changes

Reality becomes yet another facade,

The actor matures through stages

Playing roles both good and bad …

Experience doesn't annul the pact with hopes

It's deemed to be a sacrilege

To mistrust the mesmerising mirage

Even when the bubble bursts and the penny drops!…

Forbearance would bear fruits

Eventually, that is the core of his belief,

He chooses a story that best suits

His mental condition, to help him bear the grief…

The canopy is the bed where stars sleep

Alongside the souls of the ancestors,

He takes immense pride in the quantum leap

From pitch darkness to civilisational gloss…

The granary is reassuring with its plenitude,

But on the other side is the abject misery

Of fear, of being confined to solitude,

Life has the stubborn facade of congeniality…

He cannot be forgetful about his self

With the reductive vision of a myopic

There is something beyond the flesh and the fluff

The soul isn't in the picturesque…

Either everything has a meaning

Or the whole thing is a clever falsehood,

Intellectual enquiry doesn't rest, it's like a bee-sting

That insists on life being understood …

The mind knows, but how could the mind be known

The highly evolved languidly move in the mist

Searching for the times that've long been gone

The path is hazy and unexpected would be the twist …

Turbulent is the plane of tangential thoughts

Unwilling to reconcile with the pale faced reality,

Man feels helpless amongst the sacrificial goats

Melancholic is the unfree prisoner since antiquity …

The traveller is familiar with the routine

As the jet prepares for the final lap,

But enthralling is the dreamy scene

When homeland is revealed on the map!

The dream is the language of the soul

That seeks redemption through soliloquy,

What has been lost and loved most of all

Even after eons would be missed dearly …

The travel unravels the travesties of life

The faces tell tragic tales, yet full of hope,

The dream dissects the mind with its knife

As the powerful wheels grind to a stop …

The tyres are gracing the tarmac

Rocking the sleeping body to wakefulness,

The sun drenched sands welcome back

The visitor, waking up to the motherly caress…

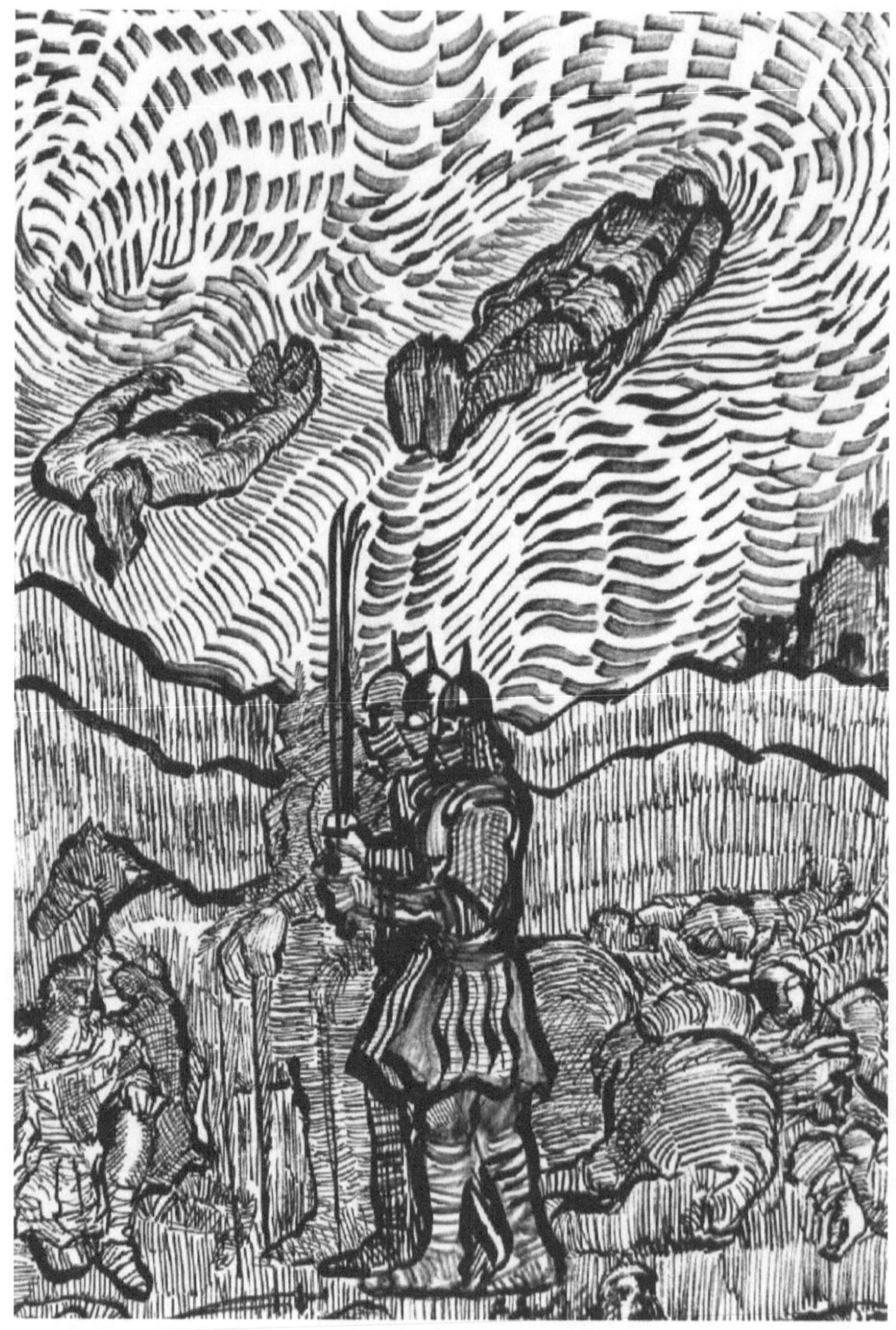

VAINGLORY

The most ancient of wars

Was between the human clans

That would leave unhealed scars,

Casting fearful darkness over the lands

From the smoky clouds of the souls

Displaced from their earthly lives…

The endless wars, the death tolls

The visceral hatred and the war cries

Are totally alien to the slain

No longer do they feel the pain

Of the injured enduring the suffering

As they have ceased to be living,

The posthumous conferring of laurels

Are mere objects like dead flower petals,

The epics speak of women ululating

Over the bodies of the dead warriors

The bards from their tents would sing

Emotional eulogies for the lost heroes,

The sculptors would spend sleepless nights

Carving the statues, to be erected with rites

By the king as a befitting monument

Covertly for his own aggrandisement!

Man belongs not to the earth, but to a territory

That's the essence of the human story

He who lays down his life for the land is brave

He would do everything that he could to save

The piece of land from invasion by others

Thus paying obeisance to his forefathers …

The clash of the clans continues with ferocity

In a violent torpor, with no scope for sobriety;

The war hero becomes the stuff for the legend

Of being undead, the valiant one's life doesn't end!

But he who has turned into a heap of dust

Has no time for the cruel worldly jest

He only had the earth, there was no paradise

After death in the mirage of the skies …

The orchestrated vicious cycles of violence

Through successive generations grow more intense

Leaving no possibility for the light of peace

As the cold bodies decay under the wreaths …

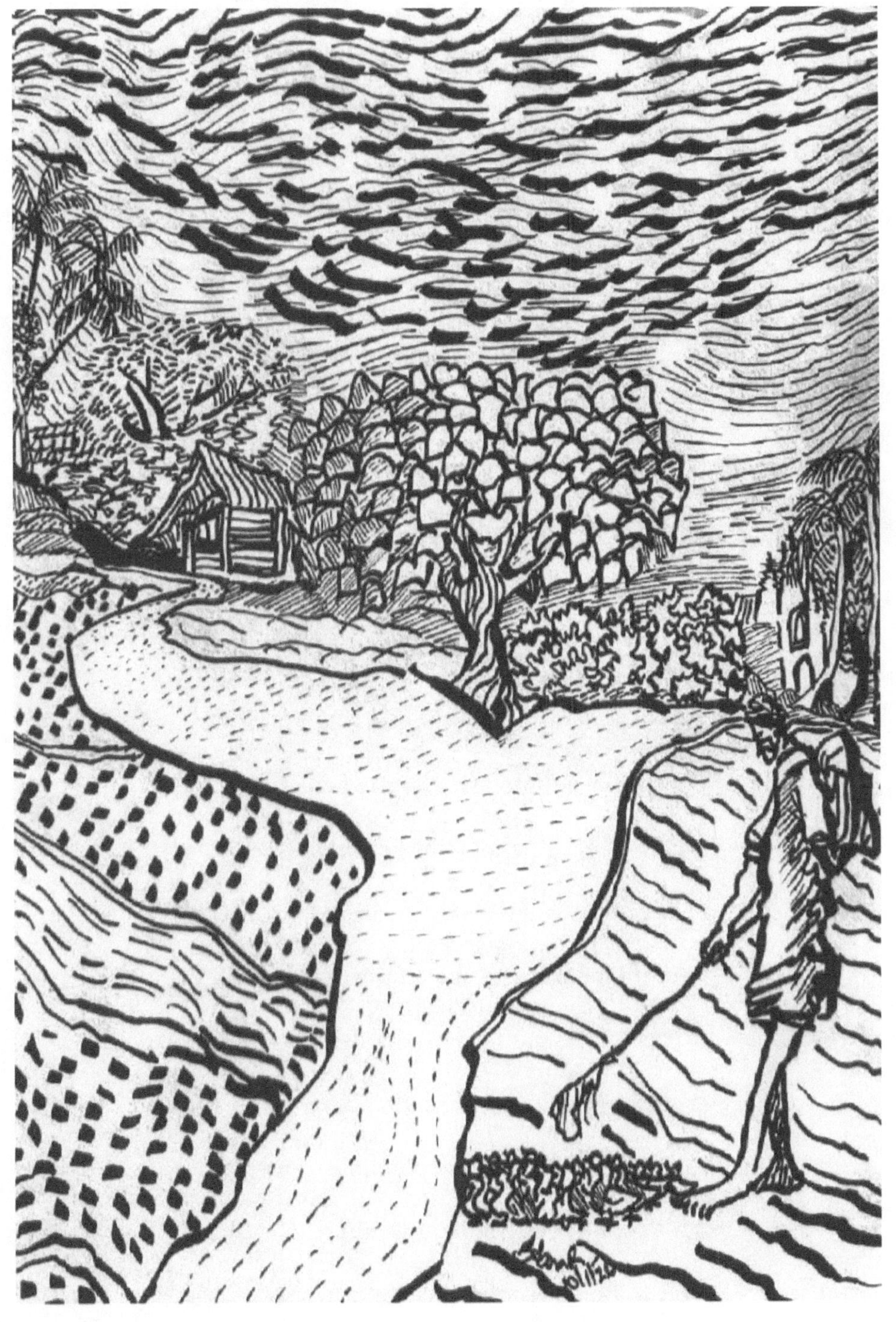

WHERE TO?

Why did I think about the park today?

I don't know for sure!

The place where it's all green

With nest-less birds and fidgety squirrels

The air with a fenestrated veil of serenity

Close to the urban jungle, yet feeling remote

And thriving within the garb of silence

Only occasionally broken by the cries

Of an antique outdated animal

Mistaking it for mysterious wilderness!

It must some form of a sanctuary

For the lost souls, this verdant place

That cannot forever stay lively and green…

Yet the bench that sits empty on its own

Has a welcoming leafy shade above it,

For the character, masked and nameless,

To bear the harsh experience of life

Not to get scalded by vain tears

Or to be blinded in the fire of reality…

Every lonely pace entices the soul

As it requires peace as its only abode,

Farther from the bitterness of existence

To couch on the grass of remoteness,

To quickly forget and to be quietly forgotten

As a weightless particle of little relevance,

Slowly sinking in the music of quietude

Where every grass blade and every flower

That cannot breathe the air freely anymore

Amidst the clouds of withered leaves,

Would eventually come to rest!

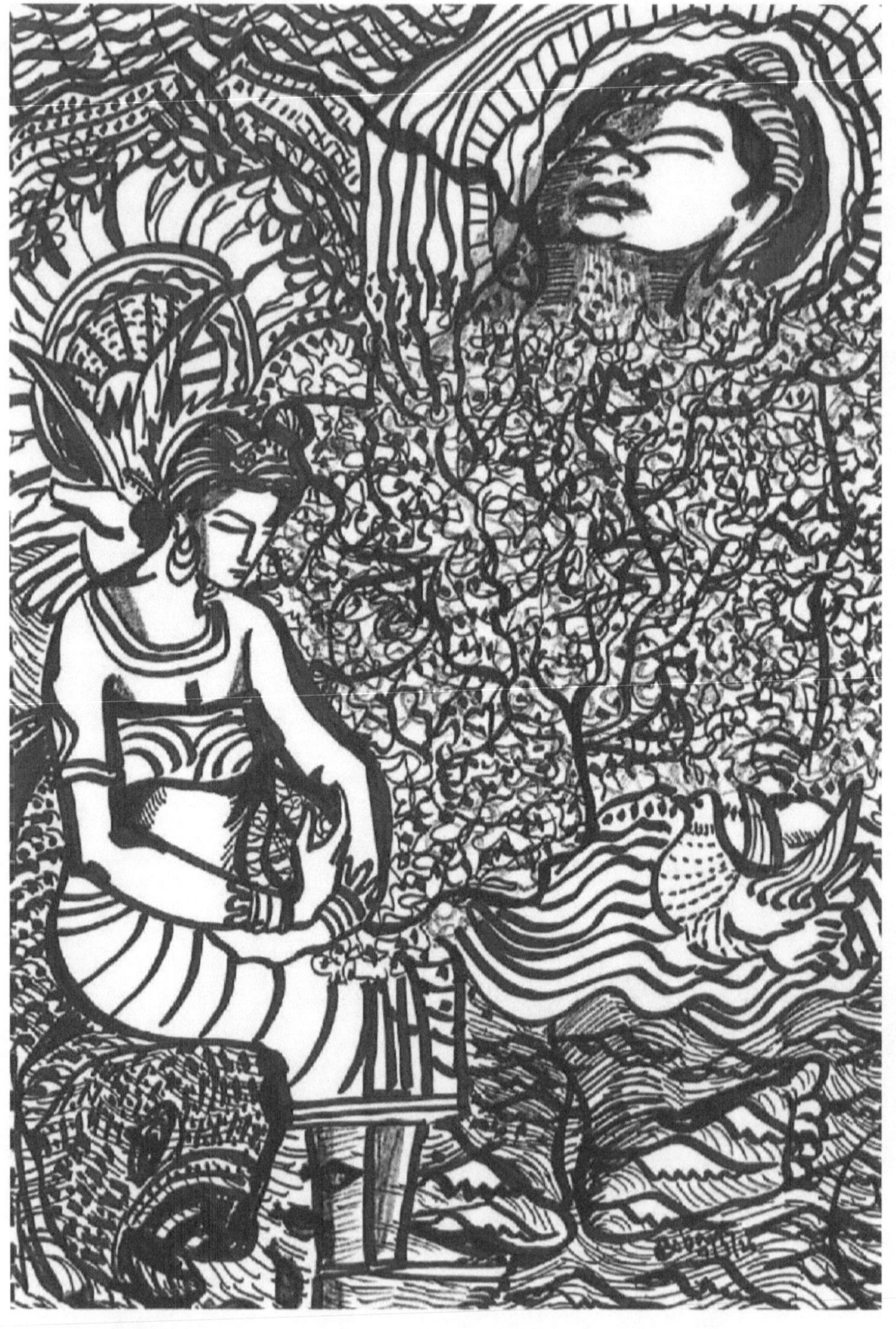

MEMORY

Why did I think about the park today?

Memories are delicate and sugary

The momentary ants take many dips

Into the pot hidden within the mind

To relish what is left behind

By time, the sweet nectar drips

From the spring blooms of memory …

Even melancholy becomes bittersweet

As time elapses, the gaps are bridged

By wishful thoughts and unfulfilled hopes,

That is how the man on earth copes

With the loss of the things he loved,

The falsification is passive and discreet …

Man needs a wall to shield his rational fear

Of invasion by age, memories are salvaged

To be the bricks, cemented by nostalgia,

He has a self-prescription for insomnia:

To be blanketed by dreams that are staged

So that he sleeps and life is easier for him to bear …

Memory is what he lives for, it's his lifeline

When the world becomes hazy and complicated

Sweetness is what he likes, it's his natural instinct,

When his faculties gradually become defunct

And the vision of the future is obliterated

Memory is his heavenly refuge, a goldmine …

Imagine the flies caught up in the web

Waiting to be devoured by the spider

All earthly lives are entrapped within fate

In advanced years, memory is the soulmate

Of man, as he waits for the natural predator

The arrival of death draped in the grim garb …

In the memories of the living are the dead

It isn't known if the dead retain any memories

Sweetness is probably needed only when alive!

The mind stores images even when it does grieve

Over loss, the repository of all sorrows and glees

Retains the memories of all that has ever been loved …

Man ought to live with the pain of memory

That serves as the reminder of his past

And the universality of impermanence,

The nostalgia could be poignantly intense

Yet he bears the pain, for the times that've been lost

Are inevitably ingrained in the human story …

The actors change with the passage of time

The narrator of dreams senses he's alone

He's the reclusive keeper of memories,

From the stash of images there would rise

A dream at night which shows a new morn

Inverting the reality to showcase the days in his prime …

Life has always been a race against time

Like a boy striving to reach home before dark

The path in the woods is staggeringly long,

Quite easily the signposts could go wrong

With anxiety the mind starts to run berserk

He panics, it's a cliff and its endgame!

The panic stricken mind relishes the fruits

In the orchard of memories, keeping the flame alive

Hopes are rekindled by the sweetness of nostalgia,

While the world throws him into a state of paranoia

Memories barricade against depression, to help him survive

He finds solace in searching for his roots…

Memory is a survival tactic for the tormented soul

Irretrievable are the days that've been lost

But the dreamy night harbingers a new dawn,

The golden rays touch the body in the night gown

Caressing him like a suckling in the nest

He feels revitalised, though on his health the days take a toll …

The souls pass on to another stratum of memory

Within the conscience of the universe

Every life carries with it a gist of the living experiences,

The realm is beyond the human senses

The path is long winded, the fog is too dense

Man cannot see what's beneath his earthly story …

Memory is the bridge between the living and the dead

It is what instigates man to envisage heaven and hell

The images populate the mind bonding him with the unknown,

The day brings new memories like dew drops on the lawn

They would faithfully stay back in the spring well

Of the mind, to fill in the spaces that've been left unsaid...

The sprites appear in the abandoned garden,

So do mermaids in the forgotten pond

As memories are suffused into the dreams,

Life's resplendent behind the sunbeams

In the realm of invisibility the souls abound

Bewilderingly imaginative is the memory of man ...

The sea roars in a fit of madness

or is it a true display of life's turbulence ?

In between the shores of dreams and reality

Is the silent coral reef of memory?

In which transient life puts much of its credence

Hidden is the shore from the superficial sphere of awareness ...

Memory is put to rest by the passing time

The images turn misty, the stories deftly rewritten

it is an adaptation of the mind for survival,

Childhood undergoes a period of revival

In old age, it is the most precious treasure for man,

It is true that he weeps over the nursery rhyme...

The mind puts up a resistance, against forgetfulness

Minting newer layers in the story of the yesteryears

Memory thus evolves with advancing age,

Man doesn't read his book of life page to page

He only wants to revisit what endears

Himself, that's his reply to times unkindness…

Memory is the wall of defence

Of evolution to combat the truth of death

The soul is said to remember only his afterlife

As unknown to him is his earthly life,

Once life passes away, what happens in the aftermath?

To the wall of memories? Does it have a renaissance?

The encapsulation of the given moment

Is a memory, and countless such would form the mass

That is supposed to end with the man,

It is an old film roll in the can

With grainy images defying forgetfulness

The building bricks of the human monument…

What would man be like with his memory erased?

He's alive, biologically, but he's dead in another sense

His new world would be a confabulation,

Through his memories man seeks emancipation

From the shackles of time, to some far off lands

That do not exist, that's what he dreams in his bed …

From the sweet aroma of milk filling the cradle

To the sweat and sebum of adolescence

Memory is a fantastic world of sensory experiences,

In its search for lost times the mind is relentless

To capture what is left of the transients

Attempting to fill the missing pieces in the riddle …

The world in itself is one singular memory

With multiple elements filling the space

The light reflected by the dead star is a living image,

Entrapped within the mysterious earthly cage

Man etches images he doesn't want to erase

That's his inner space that doesn't seek any glory …

The dog recalls his roots through olfaction

Likewise unique threads exist which link humans

To the platform of memories that are out of sight,

The remains of the day are interred in the night

What's hidden the subconscious would enhance?

As a projected dream till disembarkation…

The unseen memoir is written by the mind

To be read only by the discerning eyes

In the loft are the images of art,

They're created till death does man apart

But through memories a new world would arise

The vivid poignant images that the soul has signed …

Does man pick and choose memories for his shelf?

They're poetic reflections of his soul

The imprints left behind in his lifetime,

The identity of his soul is not in his name

The elements that make him whole

Are in the memories shelved within himself…

In the well of memories, the man-child sleeps

His heart pained by thorns of unrequited love

His yearning for permanence at odds with the reality,

The journey of the soul is towards infinity

There's no distinction between "then" and "now"

Yet the past is special for which a deep affection he keeps …

Sleep is kind to the body, relieving the stress

The night was silent, unlike the polyphony of dawn

The past sleeps while the present stays awake,

The bygone times nothing can bring back

Were indeed happier, when he never felt being alone

Moving forward brings man into existential distress …

Whilst asleep everyone is innocent like a child

Wakefulness opens the doors of chaotic adulthood

Childhood was not a trifle, it was everything,

It was the garden rich in blooms in spring

When the air was peaceful and life was good

The eyes well up when the memories are in high tide …

On the lone shore he sits on the seagrass

The waves speak the language of the heart

Nature closely reflects the state of the mind,

Worldly life compels the man to go blind

For a while, he's and adult dutifully alert

Concealed would be his memories of loss…

In a meditative state he realises the truth

As memories surge into his consciousness

Profound is the loss of those golden days,

The bird sings and the poignance it relays

Permeates the enveloping fog though it's dense

Resurfacing are the memories of being a vibrant youth…

The sunshine brings forth life as the day is born

The mind has the mine of gold, of untapped memories

Ageing is unstoppable, so too is the train of thoughts,

In the fertile flower beds in the garden pots

Imagination revitalises what time has tried to erase

The images survive though the days have long gone …

The rain paints the plants a deeper shade of green

As if their silent thoughts are being reflected

Do they have memories, encapsulated in time?

Thoughts on the trivia of the past aren't cumbersome,

To the soul a lightness is imparted

As images emerge from behind the living scene…

To the father, his grown up son is a newborn

The image in memory dominates his love

It is his altered reality, a picture he treasures!

In truth life seeks the enticing greener pastures

Adulthood demands one not to wallow in the memory groves

In his childhood he must not sojourn…

What he self-denied once, he would come to repent later

Being a man meant he had to be without sentiments

As the tide turns, he looks back at the lost lands

With sadness, the sun used to be in the palm of his hands

Memories are distant like stars in the firmaments

They aren't mortal, made of impenetrable matter …

Man is vulnerable to the gashes of guilt

Time flies and he flies alongside as a bird

In his nest he sinks into the whirlpool of emotions,

He recalls passing through many stations

He was passive, to search the truth he hadn't dared

As he believed that life was complete being an adult …

That it was just another stage, he came to realise

The memory of childhood is dearest in old age

As life fizzles out,what happens to the cherished memory ?

Moments are lively but they are transitory

The dead man has no ears for the dirge

The guest has left after having his earthly slice …

Memory is another eye of the human mind

That opens to the timelessness of life

The days are irrelevant, only the moments matter

Even if they have been perceived as bitter,

When one gets old and the joints get stiff

All he has got are the memories left behind …

Life rejuvenates itself through the transience

Sorrow accompanies death, as does happiness in birth

Memory is poignant, as it is a symbol of loss,

Beautifully arrayed like the petals of a rose

Is every memory, with nuances of the trodden path?

The feelings are deep keeping reality in abeyance …

History is a distillation of human memory

Most of which is naturally undocumented

Each grain of sand is a modicum of a civilisation,

Search for the remains with love and compassion

And one would find the faces of those who once lived,

The entire earth is a cemetery …

The habitat is thus a memory-museum

Where newer knowledge meets the wisdom

Of old

Memory is a showcased piece imbibing elements from both,

The superfluous worldly life is a changeable cloth

It's transitory, yet a beauty to behold

There is more beneath it, unassuming and sublime …

The chaos appears like a madman's dream

Born from the prejudices of unkempt minds

The violence and carnage too are parts of human memory,

The product of the inept aspiring for glory

Such memories are vocal, reverberating across the lands

They're dark clouds engulfing a world appearing grim…

That which is sorrowful stays for long

It's almost a constant, unlike the exultation

The latter lightens the heart, the former makes one think,

In a war torn nation what would its poet ink?

His hopelessness is not an aberration

But a natural response, as memory becomes a painful song …

In remembrance of love man lives

Though his life is littered with wounding trials

Hope abounds, though a distant memory is peace,

It's violent and brutal, but hopes do not cease

Optimism blooms in the countless hearts in jails

It is by trusting oneself that man ultimately survives…

Memory of images, and of words, and many more

It's more than the sum total of sensory experiences

Where is man in the collective memory of nature?

Who retains the genetic grammar of every creature,

The heart is full of regrets, forgetfulness cleanses

Making space as there are many memories to store …

Man is destined to live within the memory of another

That's how he defies the finality of his fate

His offspring carry the memory of his genetics,

Civilisation is built on countless such bricks

Man leaves a trail even after crossing infinity's gate

As he sleeps in peace under the overgrown heather…

This moment is gone, it feeds into the next one,

The chain extends to infinity, the past and future

Are reflections in the mirror of consciousness?

The memory of the future is the prescience

Of which only the depths of the subconscious is aware

Meditative in deep thoughts is the seemingly dead stone…

The mighty emperor rests in the rock grave

Unseeing everything he had once conquered

His memory is in the edicts forming the remnants,

In the ancient temple are the pilgrims' chants

Seeking penitence for every human deed

Memories adorn the walls of the universe, which's a cave…

It's not an object, yet it is tangible

Memory isn't matter, but has its own space

As the tributary of human intellect,

Amongst the many a few he would select

To relive again, the memories glow with a radiance

That would make them truly irresistible…

The father and his daughter have memories

Of their own,

Apart from the shared cache of experiences

Bonded by blood and love, the two cherish unique images,

From the same book of life they read different pages

Each one having a different take on the incidents

There isn't a memory that belongs to none…

Life is lived to weave memories together
In a finite space, the train of reminiscences
Shuttles man between the present and past,
What has faded into oblivion he would adjust?
With familiar pictures appealing to his senses
The bird desperately clings on to its last feather …

The butterfly leaves its colours to after-life
To be mused over by the human mind
It remains a vibrant memory in a life too short,
The cache of images is all that one has got
In a world that is often cruel and unkind
Till his heart stops he would keep them safe …

The dream is akin to a painting
Beneath which is the charcoal sketch
That's the outline of memories, fleshed out with colours,
Life is turbulent, through memories man endures
From memories the dreams would hatch
Many a beautiful fledgling …

After the short sleep is the languorous inertia
When the memory of a dream is pondered over

It was candid, with words still echoing in the heart,

The world is a giant wall of dream art

There are layers of meaning beneath that cover

That man strives to decipher before journeying to dementia …

The shape of memory is the sartorial choice of the mind

Stitched together with moments of love and loss

The journey is long, the traveller reminisces for his comfort,

Many an image the passing time would distort

But like the grave with mortal remains beneath the moss

It is there in the realm of reality for him to find …

It is imperative that he should find that inner space

Where memories are interred, to search for the truth

His soul demands it, otherwise his life is not worth living,

In memories man seeks the trueness of his being

He aspires to be a butterfly and not a moth

That has been his dream since the ancient days …

His soul doesn't need any words of scriptures

Art and poetry make him feel replete inside

Both of which are borne out of memories,

From the world one day he would get his release

The dark room where all his life he had stayed

Would bear the proof of his existence as pictures …

Life has an innate warmth and vitality

That perhaps only the little child is aware of

The reason why childhood memories are so joyful!

For every event memory is formed as a rule

The memento is showcased as the proof

That man did exist within the limits of his mortality …

The mind absorbs the essence of mundanity

Like a poet finding subjects in life's trivia

The scattered images create a sense of poignance,

In loneliness he introspects by availing his own lens

Going through the collection in his museum of nostalgia

Which is his isle in the sea of humanity …

Memories aren't just cherishing the joyful moments

Man is bound to relive his loss and trauma

He has recollections that he would never forget,

He remembers the words when he last met

With his dear friend, he recalls all the drama

He has been through, memories are relentless …

There is an inner urge for reinforcement of memories

Even without his awareness, it's an endless cycle

That revitalises itself through the neuronal circuits,

Man has no inkling about life's routes

Uncharted is the terrain, the body is fickle

The mind is a hive and thoughts vibrant like the bees…

Would every man care to read his inner journal?

That chronicles the highs and lows of his journey?

Only if he's brave to face the mirror of solitude,

Memories support him through the melancholic mood

When the waves are highly turbulent in the sea,

He withdraws into the space that's liminal …

The psyche is at the core of existence

With caverns unexplored, the walls echoing murmurs

Of an ocean beyond the mortal's sight,

The memory of ancient life is revealed at night

Through a dream,figures formed from the vapours

Fill the space along with images in abundance …

The memory is a story of human resistance

To the paradox of time and the reality of mortality

A parallel word is thus created on the planet,

The fish fights back from within the net

To get back to the sea, man knows his fragility

He protests against the irrevocable senescence…

The mystic says that the earth is knowledge

Whilst the universe is wisdom

Life is transiting somewhere in the interlude,

With his intellect man tries the best he could

To understand what would become

Of his soul in after life, unseen is what's beyond this hedge …

Intertwined inseparably are the old and new world

They're shared memories preserved in time

The perceived world is a fusion of dreams and memories,

The collage that is imbibed by the human iris

Is all that a mortal's soul can claim?

From this life, through which thoughts expand manifold …

Wordsworth pens words about the daffodils

That he chanced upon while strolling along the bay

A poem is a thoughtful recollection of an event,

The mind weaves a picture though it is silence

An ode to the beauty of memory

The blank paper awaits the colour pencils!…

How painful is the memory of wars

The sights of bodies pulled out of rubbles

The little graves of children buried with their dreams …

The victims of warmongering adults' tantrums

The survivors shelter within fragile bubbles

Of hope, fated to live with bleeding scars …

Are there voices from beyond the graves?

With thoughts on lives with unfulfilled desires?

The soul could be the core of human memory,

That forms the essence of life's mystery

The embers remain after the extinguishing of the fires

In distant cosmic isles lighting up the caves …

The earthly life is the memory of the cosmos

Since when did the clock begin to tick to infinity?

For, from infinity everything was born,

The perception of the mind is the new dawn

Light has always been there, lost to human visibility

The happenings recur, man keeps searching for a cause…

Man expands into the memory of the embryo

After his biological death, to be the cosmic particle

His life is archived somewhere unbeknownst to him,

Whereas in life he's full to the brim

In afterlife he's as weightless as a ripple

In natural silence does the river of life flow…

Everything changes, with such amazing rapidity

The mind absorbs, keeping some mementos

The night follows the day and the world rests in darkness,

Man avoids the signs that could be ominous

He imagines vague figures of nameless foes

While trusting the lucky charms for serendipity …

A share of the occurrences in life is stored

The undying memories keep the spirits alive

He remembers some of his oneiric excursions,

Life perhaps doesn't teach any lessons

But in the deep blue sea when he would dive

As a soul, he is seeking the memory of God …

He dreams of the beauty of nothingness in eternity

And seeks the reflections of that on earth

The mind is the vast sky, the thoughts are clouds,

The bird melodiously recalls its memorised sounds

The flaming embers are alive in the hearth

Instigating the journey towards the doors of infinity …

Imagine all the world was kind and joyful

With no brutality of man or calamity in nature

What shape would the memories have taken?

The negativity that resides firmly within men

is as important as positivity for the stature

As the wise species, existential anxiety is a vital tool …

Man remembers the festivities as well as with the wars

His heart has space for extremes of both

Memories are birthed and nurtured with equal portions,

The train has journeyed through so many stations

Much has been seen and heard since one's birth

Before the soul sets out to see what's beyond the stars …

The unassuming childhood was his safest haven

Memories latch on to the window sills and cornices

Glowing in the gold of light from the old world,

The fireplace is cozily warm, the winter isn't cold

Life feels nothing short of heavenly as he reminisces

About those days that time has stolen …

The dream has a vibrant drama within its layers

A flamboyant display of actors delivering dialogues

The audience in the amphitheatre laughs heartily,

In time the scene is a prospective memory

A living image amongst the dead bogs

The answer for enduring vitality that tops the man's prayers …

The moment is built from randomised images

The atoms of thoughts are united by unknown bonds

Creating a realistic scene that may well be remembered,

There are many such images which have been interred

In unmarked graves where silence abounds

Only a few make it to become a memory over the ages …

The reason man has a memory is never to forget

What's good and bad in his life on earth?

It's an adaptive coping skill by the evolved brain,

But forgetfulness is real, though one may feign

That he remembers everything since birth

Memory is subjective and selective, like a fishing net …

The toddler runs gleefully in the park

With a vitality unheeding the catastrophe of war

Life's simple and good, the memory is beautiful,

It has a realism that touches the soul

That scene is from another era that seems to be afar

But in the young mind it has left an indelible mark …

Life is a process, an experiment with reality

That's unpredictable due to the many variables

Ineffable is a light family moment at dinner table,

The toddler finds meaning in his own babble

Likewise man seeks moral lessons in the fables

The most intriguing being the condition of humanity …

The mind yearns for stability, without the steep falls

The constructed memories are intact pillars of support

That would keep life going against the odds,

In the garden memories grow in the flower beds

Carefully nurtured with many a dreamy thought

When the world goes dark, the bloom enthralls …

What "really" sits atop the height of fantasies?

He wonders, intriguing is the thought of what lies beyond

The distant memory of a dream is too real,

Just like the happenings in life that occur piecemeal

Like a hermitage calm the surface of the pond

But beneath it is a world of undecipherable intricacies …

Man ages with time, so do his memories

The grainy images make them more poignant

Unlike the clock he would sit still in contemplation,

He comes to realise after his meditative session

That though grown up he's still an infant

He has many things, but nothing that is really his …

The conscience is aware of the impermanence

But accepts the sensory impacts of the ephemera

The dreamer is active, he is the silent narrator,

The essence of the visuals is restored for later

He knows he knows nothing but the aura

The interpretations are highly subjective to his lens…

DR. BOBAN RAMESAN

16/03/2026

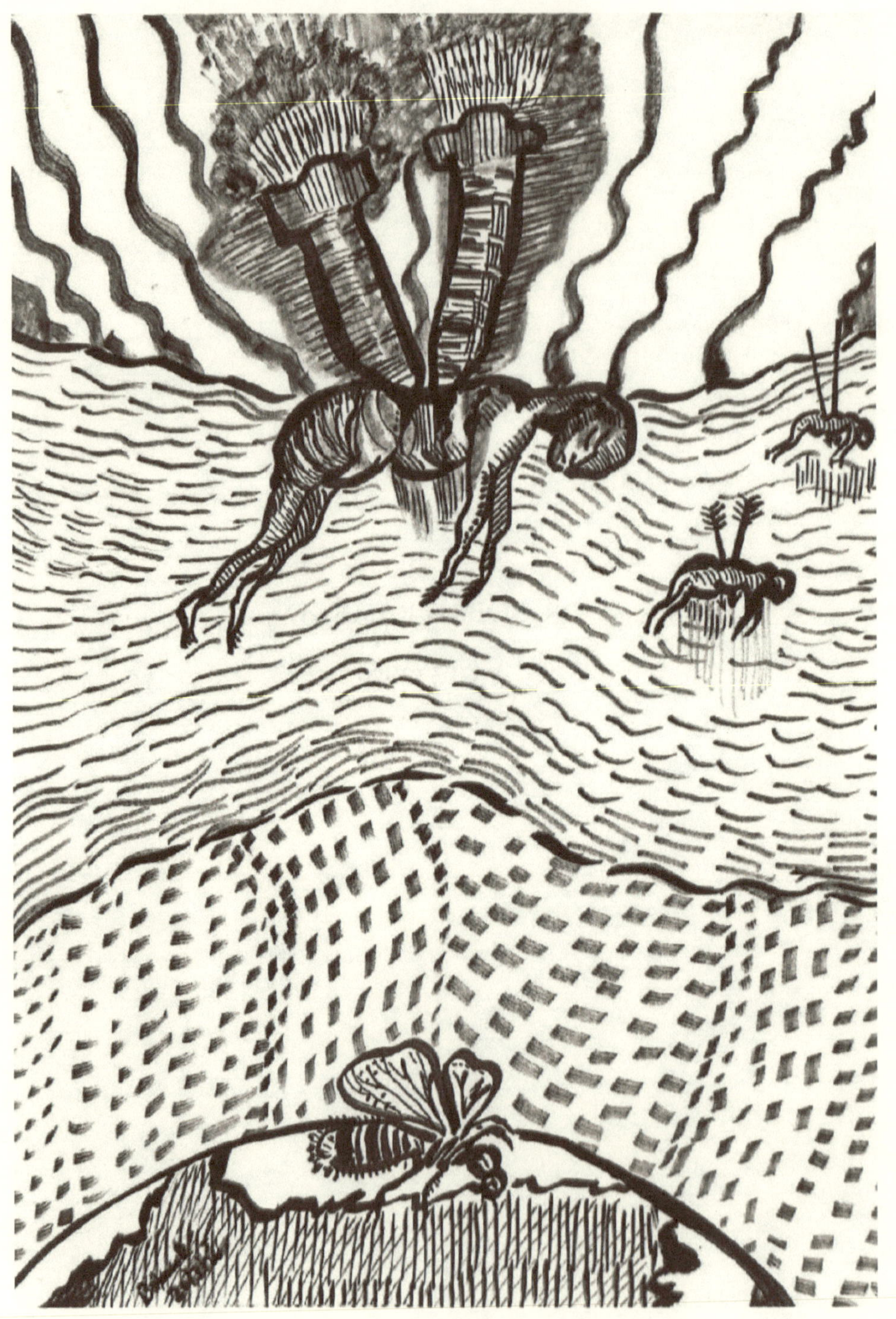

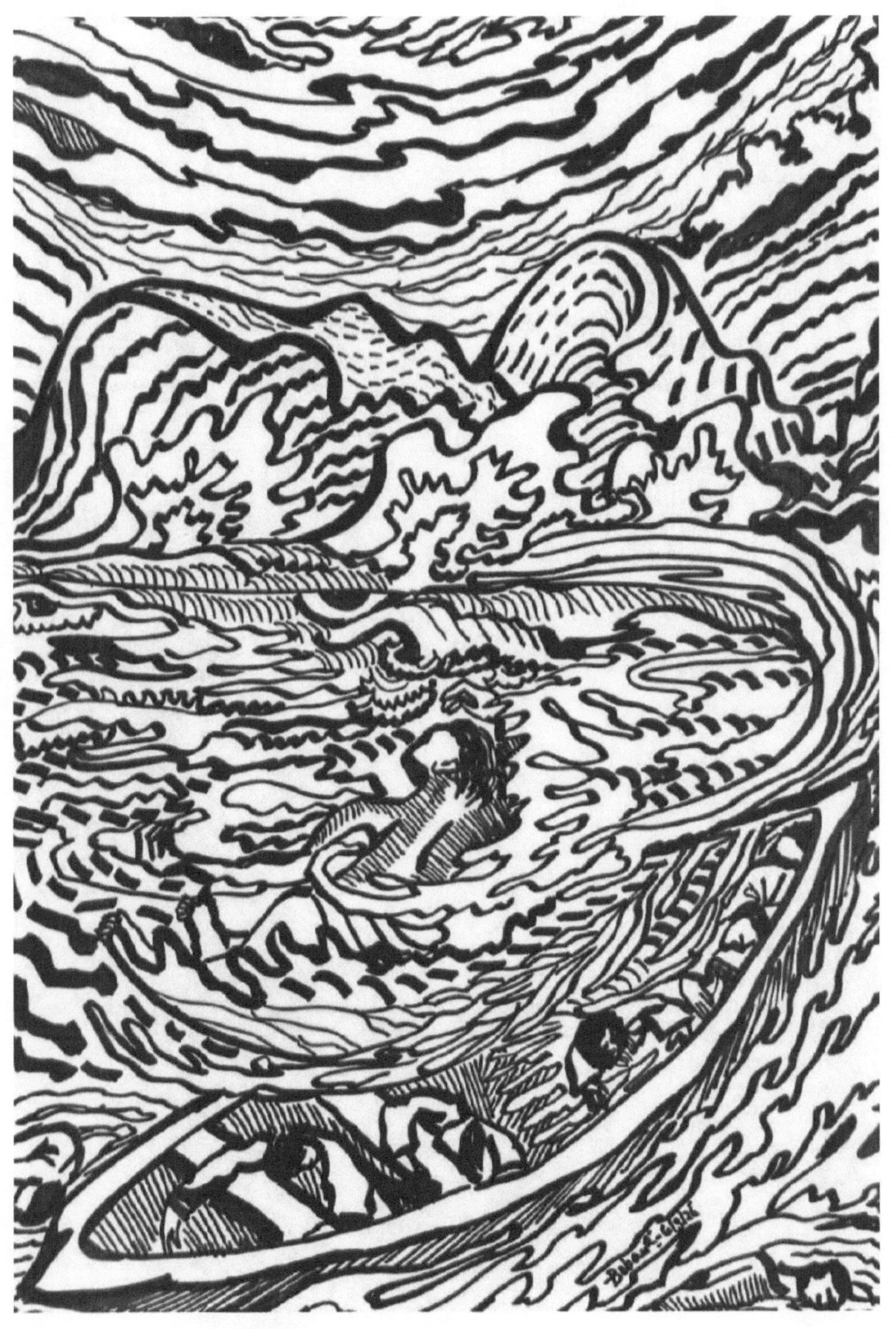

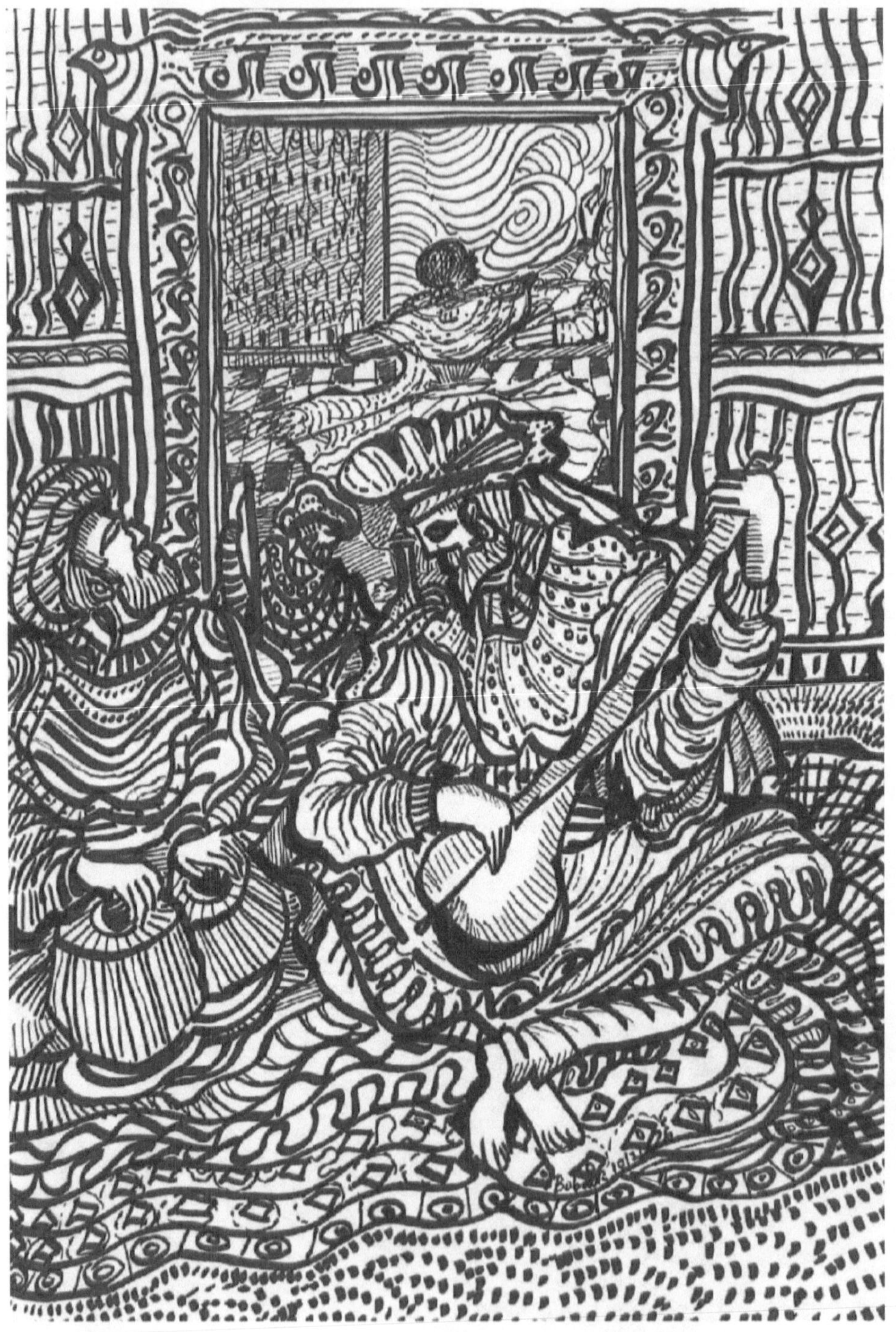

ABOUT THE AUTHOR

Dr Boban Ramesan is a family physician based in Brisbane who has a penchant for art and literature. He was born in 1977 in Kerala, India and completed his postgraduate training in the United Kingdom where he worked as a family physician before relocating to Brisbane in 2015 with his family. He has published two volumes of poetry and collections of philosophical essays in India and has conducted multiple art exhibitions which have been critically acclaimed. His poetry has influences from the narrative styles of Edgar Allan Poe and William Blake and he is also an ardent admirer ssof the works of the English romantics. To him his literary journey is essentially a philosophical quest, he finds his poetic endeavours self-explorative with the surrealistic dreamy subtleties instilled into his art works thereby creating a fascinating cycle of synergism. He believes in the poetic side of Impressionism infusing the imageries of spectacular vibrancy of nature in the eternal mystery of the human condition unravelling novel fascinating facets of the beauty of life, a collaborative union of poetry and art that effectively brings forth another sub-genre of literature.

As the adage goes

"If life doesn't have a meaning

art most probably has one !...".